" it is a Book

Love Austin

August 1987

THE RÉSTING BĚLL

Books by Anthony Barnett

A marriage
London, Nothing doing in London, 1968

Poems for the daughter of Charles Lievens
Humlebæk, privately printed, 1970 [1971]

Fragile & Lucid [folio]
Oslo, Nothing doing (formally in London), 1973

Poem About Music
Providence, RI, Burning Deck, 1974

Blood Flow
London, The Literary Supplement, Nothing doing (formally in London), 1975

Titular I-VI
Pensnett, Staffordshire, Grosseteste Review Books, 1975

Fear and Misadventure / Mud Settles
London, Ferry Press, 1977

Blues that Must not Try to Imitate the Sky
Cambridge, Lobby Press, 1978

A cowfoot
London, Curiously Strong, 1978 [1979]

Quiet Facts
London, Many Press, 1979

Report to the Working Party. Asylum. Otiose [preceded by] *After*
London, Nothing doing (formally in London), 1979

A White Mess
Nice, The Literary Supplement, Nothing doing (formally in London), 1981

Moving Buildings [folio]
London, *Lamb*, The Literary Supplement, 1982

A Forest Utilization Family
Providence, RI, Burning Deck, 1982

Poland's Neighbouring Cottage [card]
Canterbury, Epistle of Lamb, 1984-5

North North, I Said, No, Wait a Minute, South, Oh, I Don't Know (148 Political Poems)
Lewes, privately printed, distributed by Allardyce, Barnett, 1985

with David Nash
Forest Poems Forest Drawings
London, Ferry Press, 1987

*Some of these books are published in Norwegian and French translations
as books or in reviews*

Translations

*From the Norwegian of Tarjei Vesaas
From the French of Anne-Marie Albiach, Alain Delahaye, Roger Giroux*

ANTHONY BARNETT

THE
RESTING BELL

AGNEAU 2
ALLARDYCE, BARNETT
PUBLISHERS
London · Lewes · Berkeley

Agneau 2
imprint of
Allardyce, Barnett
Publishers
Established in Edinburgh

Anthony Barnett, Editor · Fiona Allardyce, Publisher

London · Lewes · Berkeley

Distributed in the United Kingdom by
Allardyce, Barnett

Distributed in the United States of America by
SPD Inc

First published in 1987 in a clothbound edition
and as Agneau 2 Paperbook 4

Printed in the United Kingdom by
Whitstable Litho Ltd Kent

British Library Cataloguing in Publication Data

Barnett, Anthony
   The résting bёll.
   I.   Title
   821'.914   PR6052.A68

ISBN 0-907954-06-5
ISBN 0-907954-07-3 Pbk

Contents

Author's Note   8

A marriage (1968)   9
Poems for the daughter of Charles Lievens
(1970[1971], Revised)   13
Poem About Music (1974)   27
Blood Flow (1975)   45
Titular I-VI (1975)   75
Fragile & Lucid (1973)   81
Fear and Misadventure (1977)   85
After (1979)   99
Mud Settles (1977)   107
A cowfoot (1978[1979])   131
Report to the Working Party. Asylum. Otiose
(1979, Revised)   151
XV Sections   207
Seedport   219
Blues that Must not Try to Imitate the Sky
(1978)   235
Quiet Facts (1979)   243
A White Mess (1981)   257
The Pipe Organ Builders   263
Moving Buildings (1982)   289
Poland's Neighbouring Cottage (1984-5)   297
North North, I Said, No, Wait a Minute, South, Oh,
I Don't Know (148 Political Poems) (1985)   301
An Uncollected Poem   373

Index of Titles or First Lines   377

Author's Note

The Résting Běll includes the contents of seventeen separate titles published between 1968 and 1985; together with some clusters and sequences previously unpublished or printed only in part in reviews. Not included are two titles printing parts of 'Forest Poems', a work evoked on another, and incomplete, scale. Two titles are here first published in revised versions; their more glaring formal or emotive defects have been excised. A few errors in printing have been corrected in other sections of this book which have been published previously; and a very small number of amendments made. The sections of this book more or less follow the order in which they were written; and do not always correspond to that of their first publication. With certain exceptions a number of distracting notes as to sources have been omitted. It would be gratuitous to assume that a mispunctuation or a misspelling is unintentional but one word, 'sta'ler', not in any dictionary, and composed of elements in two unspeakable names, is well defined—in a translation of the poem in which it appears—as 'crystalline fury'.

The poem 'To write down what you hear' was first published in *For John Riley* at Grosseteste Review Books.

For first publication of parts of this book the author expresses his thanks to Andrew Crozier, Tim Longville, Ian Patterson, Richard Tabor, Keith Waldrop, Rosmarie Waldrop, John Welch. The author also expresses his thanks to Peter Larkin. For the present publication the author expresses his grateful thanks and appreciation to A. & C.P.B., and to Fiona Allardyce.

A MARRIAGE

(1968)

for M P

I had lost even my name and was as much a pauper in this as those exiled Jews who were not entitled to engage in the occupations of their forefathers because the Prophet could not find their names in Ezra's register.
Edward Dahlberg

Semite: to find a way for myself.
George Oppen

His
name was

come
from what

a suicide

he hadnt a
country

who loved HER
to changed his name

He became Arabic
numerals
a
count
her
unbrok
en hymen

but a
Jew
who not
lived
their
families
Koran
or Testament

meant nothing

of
Abraham common
patriarch

He could no
longer be bothered

We followed

the
cemetery

buried (a
neither here nor there)

her was beautiful

For
know
he lived

POEMS FOR THE DAUGHTER OF CHARLES LIEVENS

(1970 [1971], Revised)

PROLOGUE

she cried *Herouth*
in her other language

PRAISE

values an expedient   the coin faker
was found out   and handed a screw-cutting tool
known as a die-stock   a *good*
but indirect light

IN PEACE

he was a minor poet
and resorted to mathematics
the word moment was too rare to lose
but it wasn't enough

WE MAY BE TOLD TO GO

            girl of the sea
my fantasy   among

birds and moons that used to catch fish

     Provisions appeared spontaneously in the cupboards. And
when the child took some marmalade from a pot, it remained
as intact as before,
                    as if it were my words

RICH AND PEACHY

about what is rich
and peachy   the discovery when all seemed lost
that there were oranges in the room

that i had bought oranges earlier in the day
and not especially good

what is an   not very good orange

certainly not peachy

she also had a little illustrated field guide which listed the
most common plants, as well as useful and harmful plants,

THE OCCASIONAL MEMORY

i think i had *some*thing of
interest, i didn't know how to say it
or i didn't know what to say   again

it's impossible to finish this poem

EMOTION

after the photograph
the farmers who lived in some houses
    without adequate sanitary arrangements
we were up to the knee
on a ledge above the coals

THE SPELLING

tracks in snow

          his speech
failed

what came to the light after the photographs
were printed

he knows he'd never find another like her

THE CONTINENTAL DRIFT

Gondwanaland
or Laurasia

        intellectual similarities

with *Grigia* in something like *The South*
or *The Waiting*
          for instance

    At this same hour, all efforts having proved unavailing
and the futility of the undertaking having been recognised,
Mozart Amadeo Hoffingot, down in the valley, gave orders
for work to cease.

AND THE RED SHIFT

the sound of the pink baby
crying
        or loving

i tell myself
            she meant nothing to me

THE STOLEN ANALOGY

could we overlook the analogy

resemblances were troubling him
he said he couldn't lie

in distance

the notion of a place
or a look

he stayed away
he watched himself going by

well

almost
the back side of fable

LOSS OF CONSCIOUSNESS

working in a blue mist

she were a merry maiden

BLACK ART

the last days the trees have rooks
and the trees are not full of magpies

the trees have some magpies
and the trees have rooks

spring must have come to the snow

AN IMAGINARY CONVERSATION

if he failed to bear his responsibilities
at the time he had said he would meet her
then the universe failed

if he failed to bear the responsibilities
then the universe failed

the universe was failing continually
then the protagonist tried to stop that but secured

or encouraged its failings . . .

MAHLER'S INCURABLE HEART DISEASE

he could not bear to be parted
from me for a second

i found him lying on the floor,
terrified of losing her, that
he had perhaps lost her already

that of being Jewish

THE ARRIVAL

performance is
typical
        it includes

mistakes and a typical difference

                                        dismissed with a wave
of the hand
                        acacia shrubs

CONTINUED

we were told
            because in Russian it's the begin-
ning of the word hope, and because it's only the
beginning. Just then she thinks of asking who i

DEFINITE POEM

we would sit on the rocks

a woman who is different

though the same

we could send a letter
            enclose ourselves in pebbles
and cherish every word

                        she lay down

then he said i've written about what happened and the place
it happened in and that i suppose is the only philosophy i
could possibly understand anyway
                        except for some kind of

mathematical philosophy

ONE

    found
       the *forest*

much of it is cut

   they were
good trees for swaying

TWO

the beams lying across
the harbour

that one would imagine
they were cut for boats' masts

but telegraph (totem) poles

POEM

look across the water
to the coast

wonderfully clear after snow has fallen
though it just isn't visible while snow is falling

what occupies me here

a walk out the house
crossing the road (which is not busy)
and the beach stones
near the jetty to buy fish

or the french windows
unglazed—

this, as much as any Peaceable Kingdom
is Smith's Kingdom

it is not breakfast

POEM ABOUT MUSIC

(1974)

Commentaries 3 through 11 are an arrangement by a series imposition of 'A Round & A Canon' by Charles Olson. Travels in Arabia Deserta *by Charles M. Doughty is used in working some commentaries enclosed in Part B.*

1

A   Last of the great musicologists
views harbour, sits
by water
back of a green bench &
harbours use

2

A ROUND & A CANON & A PLAY ON

3

1   As,
it is not you who sway
has this affection for you
where the arc does not yet know which

4

A bird
all saints & recitalists,
him in my hand,
of the finest honey,
the film first,
the spitting black goose
(Black-eyed Susan)

5

what a high heat
or a splint,

6

but it is the wind
or it strikes me he knows enough
balances
He ceases to fly or to sing
(the swing does not)
such nerves
the milky way

7

2   (as the Two who shyly rule
the moment
his own careful context,
as the instant dies,

8

of his dying
in mid-air
the finest worm
hangs
Even a spoon
that this child of mine
or,
over or back,
He dies.
about to fall either way is such
off the north in the night settle
—o
as I die
those
a lovely bird of a wild human motion
to the twisting of the neck of
he fell

innocent or wise
And no reference
tried down his throat like his father,
to awake to a day to sing a day down
certainly,
in the sea
Won't do.
I cannot keep him alive,
knows too much,

9

And when he falls
consider
what a very high heart,
holding
winged or pawed,
from his own world,

10

3   his eyes
close upward,
distractedly,

11

he dies
for an instant listening
to the slightest
error

12

B   what he meant, by, o, his music, his life,
           settled, once

13

        for all

14

        he'll nightly walk
        hold her imagined hand

15

      [

                       ]

the region, . . . where the KEY- or other term, or an abbreviation, is
used, or to which a NOTE applies; also enclosing a language source

16

the flute a stick
as primitive means

17

now, for the business
of a contract about, unheard
as it should

18

considered
as a check

19

hearing and motion

20

a count

21

additive

22

sex

23

imitation

24

work

25

emotion

26

infancy

27

speech

28

call

29

. . .

30

one human to another

31

the voice is far too prominent
as if it were solo with accompaniment

32

provocation

33

abstract

34

Examination of the Garden Provides
Immediate Numerous Definitions
Of the Fauna and the Flora Resisting
Seven Haughty Notions of Literature

35

followed by a song

36

a sparrow took the swan's down

37

Stomach Does Not Lightly Stomach Membranous
Abdominal Sacs Which the Dictionary
Concord(ance) May Hinder Investigation
And Happily Old Cheese and Purple Tallow

38

O Burdened Music Bird Which Map Accordance
Maps Her Winged History All Perspective Spoke
That Burdened Plot Obtrude His Loving Hop Hop
The Crass Grass Move and Chatter Amongst Sturdy

39

O Burdened Music Bird Which Map Accordance
Maps Her Winged History All Perspective Spoke
That Burdened Plot Obtrude His Loving Hop Hop
The Crass Grass Move and Chatter Amongst Sturdy

40

O Burdened Music Bird Which Map Accordance
Maps Her Winged History All Perspective Spoke
That Burdened Plot Obtrude His Loving Hop Hop
The Crass Grass Move and Chatter Amongst Sturdy

41

free rhythm, from our animal ancestry,
an earlier quality. Strictness
comes with man

42

heartbeat
and lapse and stress
in act

43

Rose Out Tenders Innumerable Prospect
Leaves and Bees Enjoin Sun Tasks Commensurate
Bedraggled Object Retrieve Finite Quiet
Qualities Not Obey Cyclic Disorder

44

sabotage his
and her music

45

contemplate silence

46

he loved
and held back
her back
proceed another kind of snake
most black irregular
the shouts and fires,
blindly,
as a wild, and
a dismal sound
a world of lush,

and bush
grew too warm
too warm as thick
another hand,
that the old scalp was genuine

47

By the middle
were both wrong
square of skin
a crude wall
blow with its paw
slept,
kissed,
tried for a moment
watched the sun go in
soundlessly, water
preens his wing

48

A COPY
more than three lines
in pits
they can what they find a wonder
disbelieved, and imagined
in a free state

49

undoes her charm
ash of this
cleans orifices
feeds her baby

in his spirituous humour, and haughty
the sweetest of humans
when in a journey,
must lie to sleep
'solitaries'
a sterile waste
hand, worth
go then to settle remotely
a pleasant wonder
as living of their two hands
they marry not
but go on as an Arabian,
in his loose cotton tunic,
mantle and kerchief,
with naked shanks and feet,
his sandles,
he had put off at the carpet,

Hmm,
tiding
wide blown in all the tents
none can detain her
unseemly,
(a guest)
I am thy guest
the coffee pestle
and the mortars,
limestone
marble, sunna's work
All is here as we have seen
a heavy din
the old fever
sheltered,

as between walls,
fearing
to pass so open a country
appeared a dream-like spectacle
but pray,
so long as thou shalt pray
I may not compel thee

52

mild-hearted
the remedies you have
and for diseases
shuffling steps in the silent and forsaken ways
by the unpaved public place
and lodge
he would ride out of town
housewife
which is the cooking-fire
and rude son

53

fearing less
had not some secret
a schedule of safe-conduct
with better looks
but had climbed
grip
disherited
took from shoulder
and with human kindness
in that simple company

54

a little old
rotten
they storm
although so fair
upon a brow
broken
heat, of buttermilk
drenched
and mount
a vast blackness
lying as a tongue
the tongue under the palate
upon a side
leaping

55

sobs
in her vast throat
not
shift for himself
the hollow laps

56

in which
upper sand
hammer, timber yields
under border
where tender herbs nourish him
massy horns
the haunch
as from our childhood we have seen pictured

who wakens
in his rough song

57

a chorus
assemble hither
of a single verse
an angry voice

58

pitless
in battle
whom in their herding life
turned to flight
so fast
insensible wind
in a low place
lead thy parents into paradise!
You know he was sick
the night passage were safer
the negro bred
among Arab
words
and forged
a gift of sun and rain
evening promises
and at sunrise

59

relic
and learned minds

60

weary stranger
she answered
a strange look
wild man, and his fellowship
newly cleared
a shift
to climb downward
in a low ground
distant, but the rest
say their ancient
and heard the evening sounds

61

themselves by twos
and threes together
to wild
hazard
shot strikes
proportionate reach
at the ground
upon
so
long
legs
with a hostile face
one evening
so they say
'it kills people'
bereaved dam wanderers
full of tears
in households

62

place
with his finger
chapter
held and hired
withering plants
in that
not superfluous
weights
to the chain

63

in movement
song
a pestilence
in hierachy
in locked doors
antagonism
definition of love
her care

64

in the light
insects
on arm bitten
unharmed
mothers' fear
you have spoken to me badly
which is song

BLOOD FLOW

(1975)

I

WOMAN SPOKE

Very pure heart
and maybe
because—

I have lost the courage
or the ability

give her. . .   keep that
You
who must be
carefull.

(the You is I)

CRUX

The origin
was
unheeded

was born of
water drops
the ringing of bells
roped off
which dropped away

Anyway, the word, was rung,
would not be used
would never mean
nor what it would not mean.

CELAN

I did not know you
but I
well enough imagine
Do I?

Night behaviour
and dirt

into which You were fallen

You pushed.

Executor,
estranged, prayerless,

by a followed memory.

THE CITY

I think of you
Kristiania, affectionately,
I must think of you

because
you become a woman

Kristin

and you are no longer
a finished name

in springiness
of a year's snow
a year's snow

CLOISTERS

The grey friar.
Who is the grey friar?

And the black Jew.
The black-haired Jew.

Who is the black-haired Jew
alone sits

at pane of the square?

Is the Franciscan celibate?
And is the tree what it is

and what
its railings?

Does the Jew recite
at the wall?

In what language?

Where, by the way, his family.

MASKS

Celebrate
you, celebrate

thinking of

you were thinking
not

it was,
only to drink

thinking, that was
enough

I, each time
I
see a mask.

ANA

If I work back
from you:

walk back

the any-one-bridge

to the left
or to the right

or

swim
forward

depth, reach

I—

lack:

do I lack?

FALSE

Close up
circus brass.

It is the sound that
dismays

the you and I
we were.

On, talk
I think.

O, quick to the smile,
silver,
to the touch.

Engaging smile,
—it was my dismay.

THE BOOK OF MYSTERIES

Here, in the
book
of the what?

What foolishness.

How?

In rock and tree,
and, soundlessly,

what can I ask from you?

I told you,
I told you,

I formed you, the anger and the nothing that would
hold you; I, on you, hold.

THE LIE

Lie.

In the great room.

Above you.

Lie, thinking,
eye, the brow, brow.

What was done?

Was it there?

Was it killed?

Stillness terrifying
as the still.

Stillness of air, word.

You said.

You were not good to me.

You knew.

ICE, FIRE

Between—

You and I,

speaks

if it is silent,
the fingers

if it is crippled,
eyes

if it is blinded.

You are alone, I am in a loved one's arms;

to the heart-beat.

YOU SPEAK

Of

solitary mountain
song, nameless,

above
little edible leaves

that are,

I do not leave you,

in Green.

CODICIL

I, in a
house

a child, once, I saw born;
another I named.

In consequence
they are not mine.

Easily
you are
barrenness

—like a symbol.

This is my penitent.
Thus, poem is water.

I shall write:—

All darkness is
forgotten.

        You are
        a written
        berry
        . . .
        written
        as a
        berry.

II

DROPS

White
of the Northern bird—

What white?

White ice,
crystals,
besides, the
black lake, blue-gray lake,

because of the water-dark,
May sun.

Speech-like,
beside
bleak prayers of ice
breaks, before morning;

the morning
where your voice is transmitted

is silenced.

MUSEUM AND PARK

You welcomed me
before all the drawings of the city.

WITH YOU

Loss.

Thank you.
Your absence. For your absence.

Thank you for your absence.

Word.

Of stone.

SLEEP

I dream, have not dreamt.

Cradled in
hollowness.

You catch remoteness.

ORCHESTRA

I drum
the song
into you.

You do not remember the song.

TO REASSURE, TO

HABEAS CORPUS

My behaviour,
barely perceptible,
was corrected.
I
did not
know
whether to tremble
or be still.

ABSENT

My sister

clarinet
in e.

Horizontal, vertical.

Her father's daughter.

Protestant duty.

What did you tell her?
You hit her, you did not hit her.

You confused her.
Inborn.
You spited her.

In the form of
Hebrew letters.

You kept quiet about
madness.

You broke down numbers,
you saw no difference.

You were afraid.

You suffered.

My sister
was spiritual.

THE PALACE

I walked.

Dear Kristin.
I walked.
You motored by
with huge eyes.

By the real theatre
which empties.

Were you the purity?
Were you there?

The Water-Palace
helped, was almost
still, yet reluctant.

MEMORY

You hide.
I think you were
sick.
You do not want.

Unite
and untie.

Satiate ice,
you sleep earthily.

You throw out
mouths.
You throw out.
You crust.

CROSSING

Germanic.

Irreligious.

You blaspheme. You utter your God.
You are renewed
in mountains where you were lost.
You sluice
yourself with water,
untouched. You are baptised.
You remain
with
your Jewishness.

At times
you await your dying,
your adoration and birth
of another; but you remain
with your Jewishness.

DEATH

Hearse
you carry
within.

You are
feather-like
pæan,

You do not
carry
sufficient ink.

You were
young.
—You were bequeathed.

I pleaded
companionhood.

You were
white

Hearse
you carry
me
within.

You are twice
defiled.

Within
me.

APODAL STRIDE (CURSIVE)

As the mower
commences, I

jar, disrupting
empty breast.

You were sweet
enough
with rose breasts enough
to stow my curse

I am forgiven,
blood flow,
I am forgiven.

TITULAR I-VI

(1975)

SOME SCANDAL THAT HAS FLOATED DOWN
FROM HIGHER CIRCLES

By the twilight
the airy insects arrive
gathering low
so that the wagtail
appears beside me.
Likewise, the
lake-lily is hardly
permitted to remain
flat on this surface.
It is tugged at,
bowled to the dining-
table. Prematurely,
the flat leaf
will be joined by
the bud. The paraph
caught on a filament,
the pleasure cannot
be denied.

CLEARLY, AND NOT AT GREAT LENGTH

Threadbare, it bores into
the apple, touching
on the centre. The pip
is aggravated. Light pours
in through the blemish,
scorching the skin surface.
Needlessly, a precarious
house is aired. It rots,
disregarded, bruised
from the jolt, is accorded
an impartial bite,
or carelessly discarded.

MY DAUGHTER'S BROUGHT A GOOD MAN HOME

Even so, as the waddling
duck swallows bread
white as the gullet,
expectantly I round the corner.
A dispassionate velocity
tunes to the ear
as a truth or a wig.
Even so, such adornment
is admonished.

IV

Residual cover,
a neck of vests, disguised
as liberty, a disguised following,
excised, through a conning
tower. This is not
what I come here for. My real love
and I tear from cone to cone, brushes,
tusks of looseness and
aloneness.

V

The gulls cry inland; the
herring gull also focuses.
Change is heavy there
and other cries of dormant
learning follow the shore
line. We are already inland
where the shore line merges with
scarp forest.

VI

Smoke from the factory rises
across the expanse. The filter
dirtied, the key snaps off the
ignition, breaking the heart-bone.
The light dims, finally dying,
and catches the fish in mid air.

FRAGILE & LUCID

(1973)

—

You are not fragile.
I believe
you are not fragile
and do not believe
in this lucidity,
pronouncement of this fragility.

I am not lucid.
You believe
I am not lucid
and do not believe
in this fragility,
pronouncement of this lucidity.

FEAR AND MISADVENTURE

(1977)

to M P

In this
Green and Blue—
They are vast
together
holding
a white wisp
a white wisp
a white wisp
a white wisp of a cloud,
down, a wind borne seed.

I am cold.
This vastness is
quiet,
is warm-blooded,
is brought inside,
is finally distracted.

In this Green and Blue
within this vastness,
life deaths.

I am abstract
quality
I am the large fern
fanning the wood,
with no more temporal movement.

The foliage is not vast,
but its detail a vast
coinage. This is the cause,
the foreshadowing. The
offspring shaking, the curve
of the stem.

You die in this
vastness.
The feather goes
out of your hand.
In the net of a cherry tree,
cut free.
The point is, the catch
fails, and the catechism is not clear.
Fear and misadventure
mean this.

I and this vastness
are blind.
I stare or gaze
roughly.
The greatest confusion
is the line
where the views divide.
It is also resolute.

True voices
in this vastness
speak to me at twilight.
They speak to me with a blackish
look and a black pen.
True voices,
easy to lose,
yours and mine,
in this vastness.

Time is a kind
response.
Though I hear what I play.
No one accompanies
me.
What I finger I imagine,
what I hear is true.
Thus I am integral.

In Green and Blue
the day is over.
Memory is fresh as eye water.
In front of no one
I am tyrant and martyr.

Do you think I am a stone,
do you think of a mark,
do you think of a barb,
you are crossed out.
You will always be
crossed out.
You are ova far beyond
my reach.
I hunt for you, I fish
for you, I labour for you.
I tongue for you
in the crudest and most
pure manner.

The history of theatre
is that of absence.
It is unsound.
It is not wanted in this,
where climate would be displaced.

I rub out all that this vastness
does not want.
It does not want my negligence,
or my memory of nothing.

I turn against you
and again
in this Green and Blue
it breaks you,
like a staler.

I spit orange.
My spit and an orange
was on offer, inseparable.
I am scattered by viciousness,
but the tactile viciousness of your hand
is unknown to me.

I am bound in this leaf state.
Should I recognise myself
in this day and pond light.

Victory is not subdued.
It is unmoral
and moral victory
~~has no~~, is heartless.
Defeat also.

Then light fails.

Do not imagine
in this shored up
vastness
where you lose, ourselves.
I grapple there with the dark and a line silence
disinterned i.

What is you
is closer.
What is closer
kneads me.
I hug you
and you become closer.
I forget you, turn to you.
With you, I am black,
I am dew, the Lord.

Before this history
I shame you.
Whether I feign or learn to disregard you
you will not return.

I walk from day to day
under an immensity
that escapes me, that I do not escape.
You command resources that I do not command
but you are not resourceful.
I exaggerate as you do not.
I smart with you.
I am stopped with you.
I mix up
I go to pieces.

Your sharp stresses
are hidden.
Away from
leads to recluse.
But laughter,
distressing, unthought,
is unthought.
And then why the magpie
flies off.

The small verse
breaches
because of the enclosure,
but, not the sense.

It is troublesome to search
for you again.
The distant lamp like stars
lights you distantly.
Capillaries and veins
protect you like a cover.
I am troubled. I cover you
by heart.

The meaning of my dream
is altered.
I am tired of mistakes.
I have exorcised unopposed
opposites.
My dreams which come to nothing.
My night emission.

You are the last frame
of light, picture light,
in the dusk
in the corner of my eye
as I doze off.
I do not know what happens
in you or in me.
When I awake
nothing has changed except
appearances.

I lean across you
in this Green and Blue
out of my heart's Godness
and salt our sand with snow.
In May the ground relates
September twice with futility.
When I lose you
I take on your character
and lose you.
I give you the choice
of a corkscrew.

The ferry boat comes out of the mist fast.
It is made fast to the bollard at the quay
and rocked by the wash of a liner.
The gangplank shifts
and people about to get off are held fast
in the mist.

Snow falls everyday,
and does not fall.
It is neither winter
nor summer.
I listen to your every sound.
What I think is all right
and what imperils me.
There, a falling away.
Surely, I am grown nearly,
am answerable.

You must listen to what is said.
You are spoken for,
and that is wrong.
Behave in forgetting or cognizance.
You must not guess.
You must go now.

After bloodspring
you would have thought
there would be a vast change.
He was good to us.
Why do you offer us a home
when we have done without.
She paid for a tree in my name.
That this is just a jot of the truth
is understandable.
Yet, yet, I do not understand.

How close is this wound,
that I thought would fall,
when I fell on my knee,
when I was afraid
—of vastness.
Lasting, because of my answer,
a retort,
out of place
in this between Green and Blue.
How suddenly the wound closes.
A flower would feel it so.
I got up.
I was no longer there.

AFTER

(1979)

I

I am after, but not before;
I am unsure how life is after life before.

There are wild, there are garden:
no fact comes to life

but one lifeless.
Silent em: now where are you?

I cannot find you so easily
in this garden or this wild

because you are variable
and only beginning is invariable

and because you are moveable
and beginning is perhaps immovable.

Talk, be silent, but respond.
I am like clinker.

I am consciousness of every and.
I think we make it so.

I get up. I lie down. I get up.
An impassible position.

But what do I think I have lost?
What do I think?

On seven days
God is lies, also Marx, Freud,

and the Saints, smaller saints, who had half-eyes.
It is true for you, me, and the rose,

whose half-eyes open—
and open eyes half closed.

So I cover up. It is in the sun's angle.
I think we make it so.

A polar rose modified by long shadows.
The Russian me eternal as a cat.

I swam.
I could not think of anything else.

I was definately afraid.
Where are my toes? I wondered. Where was there shade

for digging in to? A fine gap
for getting through

as in a hedgerow? Oh, I love you so.
But there are limits to this.

II

How lovely is the smell of my love's annulus:
solar rose, lovelier than the past.

Sparrows build nests under the eaves.
Their droppings wash the woodwork.

I nuzzle close to the grass.
I do not know what I have done.

Sparrows twitter below the eaves
and beneath the reed of my chalumeau.

Roses grow in the sun.
They are coloured ordinals.

The fragrance of close mown grass
is as lasting.

She is undone. I am undone.
We head for Africa.

It is not how it is.
It is and it is not.

Levels of dirt become cleanness.
Man does what man has to.

Woman is all exposed.
Fuck this, and fuck this.

It is like love
and it is not love.

Quietly, I sit squinting at the sun.
Is it a veranda or a terrace?

It is covered, a platform
at ground level, with the front entrance

and the ground floor.
Yet it is a level area cut from a slope.

Is it a veranda and a terrace?
Is it a meaningful question?

The flagstaff has splintered.
The mouthpiece of my chalumeau is shattered.

Snow is melting on the ground
and ice on the water.

I left my love long ago
when I was asked to go.

It was hard. I left ignobly.
I am sure she has not looked for me.

III

There, is a stake, I see it, now,
    which is likened to the object.

It is not true. It does not pass for it.
    But, still, is a common growth,

by not leaning on a birch,
    as in going up and coming down, is

being—supported on a leaf slope.
    I am the lizard and the belied step.

I am quite harmless, and I am dry.
    My stone is at rest.

I am not historical enough.
    I am the splayed blossom.

I finger it.
    My crystalline lens is wet.

O lizard stay!
    I am grown fond.

Holding women's babes as blacks' music,
    historicity, was, before, and, is, beside.

Thus reflexion is least expected,
    but is not defective in the object,

but in judgement.
    It must not be symbolist.

I think of the whole caste,
    and how it sticks.

How it lasts out,
    how it is reduced.

In spring we set the grass to fire.
    We wonder if small beasts scurry

into ditches.
    They do. We want them to.

They scurry across badly prepared roads,
    badly signed.

We see that now;
    that they break up under ice

and metal parts of winter tyres.
    It is like simony.

We are smoked out.
    And work not hard enough.

MUD SETTLES

(1977)

to A

Mud settles.
I was trying to keep up

to penetrate the locale colours
to affirm day to day
stillness, monotonous ineptness.

But the wind, as I awoke,
blew—
a spruce waved
and just snow dropped off
may morn.

The bush is shaped like a cupped hand.
Expansive.
Plenty berries will persist.
For the moment bees begin.
Short nettles grow unseemingly.

I am thinking about
catkins developing wind borne seeds
indoors.
Do you think for one moment
they would deliberately allow themselves to get trapped.
Oh no. They use the slightest draught.

I know this place
so well, I thought.
I was born there, and schooled there.
But matters
about which I know so little
as I went away, go back.

Scythe. You implant the long curved blade.
Behind the line of spruce, just now, you see
a girl perambulate. Straw grazes the eyes
there.

The wasp
comes in
to settle on the house.

Settle on nothing.
The wasp is beastly afraid.
Mucks about, muck about.
Seems so, not to know its job.

Muck about.

What is so strange.
What is the matter.
You are so strange.
You look at me like that.
Fellow-feeling, broken
too near the storage.

How you grow.
You are no guest,
no guelder-rose.
Light hardly alters you.
How it lasts for you.
How you go on.
At the salt lick
first how pale you are
how red you are.

A light rainfall.
A migratory bird
flies into the night

in a quick curve.
I did not see it.
How you are word blind.
I do not know *why*.

How you recognisably falter over a hyphen.
Think how this began.

Compounded of literal
speech.

I wish you would
warm to it,
like the rock face
and the water below,
be not forthright,
not devious,
but the rest.
I am not *wish*ful.
How watery my eyes are.

One light stares out,
another back,
a blackletter, unintelligible.

My fingertips dig up your sweet smells.

You hardly know it.
You wheeze a little.

Here, roughly,
the wickers.
The size and shape deficient.
But they are built in.
They are serious, at risk.

Far off
(not actually so far)
a couple waving. It burrs.
No, it is the winter wild oat
irresolute at the edge.

Since it is like a leaf,
autumnal leaf,
blown across the hard surface,
it is certainly a leaf.

But the rising heat, th' innard,
is mammalian.

The night stares out
dissolving
that which the night star doubts.

Why do I fear the symbol
of a night's gambol?

Look at the warmth of my bed.

Why should I doubt that?

Rape stalks are laid
with snow.

This is not a description.

I ask myself.
There is nothing for it.

I *am* asleep but
I *am* distressed.

What are you doing?

Dead rape stalks
are laid down with snow.

There is no deception.

The eyes startle
as they are borne so close.

It is the same.

Conflict between
what attracts
and what is already close

is suddenly so difficult.

The rose stays in the cold.

It is quite lost to all feeling.

It is a shallow grave beneath it.

The frost lets you neither in nor up there.

I am not so bold as to climb there.

When I look out on the world
am I wiser than thou?

How you delude me.

Blood dries on the hot sand.

Blood of my beloved.

But you are nowhere
to be heard.

I hear about such things.

I want to close my eyes,
if I have eyes.

They hurt.
They are carried by lashes.

It does not matter what I say.

The world is a half terrible place,
at least, a terrible place.

Who would deny it.

Lambs and the limbs of others are consumed
in plenty, with no grace.

The summer berries
are a fine sediment, now.

We smell them.

There are pheasant in the garden
and at evening
dark patches in the snow,
the smallest bushes,
are like leafless pheasant.

The dark moves like the breast
of a pheasant.

It is safe here. Here,
it is safe.

Below the field of fleshy oat
a stave kirk is sometimes
floodlit.

Stone or staveless.

I see it in the starry
or mist night.

It aspires to a state of grace.

And who worships the fleshy saviour?
And who does not ascend each spring?

I bite too hard
and a cyst forms
in the mouth under the lip.

It seems to heal
but latent, latent

I tell them I do
not want their busyness.

Either they smile
or stare.

Is it the cyst
they see?

In haste
I hardly stop to look at things.

It is as if I
had thoughts like a girl
blushing in the branches.

To take breath
and not to lose it.

Our understanding is
modified by it.

Under the light
they are swarming under the snow.
Small new flakes, not winged,
but landing and disappearing.

Picture of horror with no basis,
no morpheme.

This poem is also for you.
It is an outgoing,
a place of going out,
an upshot, an offspring,
a profit, a point,
a putting forth, the thing
at issue.

Just wipe away your issue
with a tissue.

A single crow
chooses
the highest point
to look

at the high moonlight
in the morning.

Close to an old farm.

The road is steep.

On my side
a lower tree has left
three leaves.

But they are sparrows
and not leaves.

Desert rose, desert rose,
you will find your birthday cemented,

in sandstone.

But it does not belong
only to you.

It is readily detachable.

Spines grow out
of the curvature.

It gives.

You are wet and warm.
You are so cru

Fleshy stems are reduced,
like this,

so are their lobes.

It was a crow
as you queried.

How you are an influ'
but for the good.

I altered it
and feel the crow approve
this concern for
the true.

What is true.

The crow is our friend.
The crow is maligned.

The leaves in the tea are
a premise.
The temperature is a wizened old man,
an implement to write with and be shot at.

This is the degree of dispersion.

Where is your lousy commune ethic?

Will you do anything?

Or balk.

The traffic light switches
in combinations of three,
sometimes two colours.

You cross over dreamily.

You dream of a prick
as big as a horse's.

You are an assassin
with rosetip nipples.

You are a thick part of things.

With all the care in the world
I feel things draw to a close,
though they are really far away.

If they were around us.

Where does this language
really come from?

A wise man would seek it
close to home.

I look at the two girls
who seesaw in the picture
perhaps without knowing it.

The boat in the distance
has a sail.

Is it necessary?

I see you, swimming
in the sound

while I am calm.
Forgive me.

I feel you break water
beside me,

You do not see them.

A splash of ink struck
the right phone.

I give up.

Sometimes the antonym is right.

In the track of whales singing.

It has no depth,
much remembrance, no drying.

The flow is shut off.

Shale splits.

The yellow flame surprises.

The picture is green and blue
and rocky too.

What is in the cave
is in the picture.

The yellow flame rises
out of the picture.

You are the waiter.

You are most old.

The fronds are exposed to the sun
and night air.

The cold protects you, may also
mislead you.

The room is silent.

Clouds race.

They leave a clear windy night.

A trembling at every rise.

They have followed me with their different sounds.

Go not out by night alone.

Nothing stirs.

There are marks on the macadam.

Stubble shows through the snow.

A terrible orchestra of contraction
and expansion—

if I sleep through it, it is a dream.

Oscillate.

There are many.

The sun is over there
and a dull memory

of wiry hair.

Nausea.

Coming at an end
the heaviness unloads on you.

They depend on you.

Their motion is processional.

They uncover the springs
and chant.

There is no end to it.

Even the thickest breaks

such as an ice slope.

Lesion.

Tension.

A COWFOOT

18 STOLEN SONNETS

(1978 [1979])

for A K

*The drawing in Sonnet II, 61 (77) is reproduced by permission
of the Executors of the Charles Montagu Doughty Estate.*

SONNET I, 448 (495)

Some days I sought shelter
without suspicion.
Two are the well-heads
that touched to the skin
a blister, which burns for a day or two.
Descending place.
These thick shadows
great as the palm and fingers of a man's hand
fly in to water from the dry wilderness.
They stretch themselves
upon the ground
like a falling blossom.
A man may bow himself
in the valley.

SONNET I, 495 (543)

Reach me.
Deceive me.
Besides us.
A stranger might trust himself.
A great
inroad.
Come.
Commonly multiply.
I soon fell asleep.
I awoke
upon her.
Look!
Lay here
the winter.

SONNET I, 38 (75)

A sandstone mountain appeared.
We came here to a summer camp.
An obscure tradition.
Take the country?
This honest host fed us
with milk.
Religion. It seems besides
to circumcise.
Years ago
he saw some men warming themselves in a field
and went and sat down.
He reproved their ignorance.
Old man
let him lie.

SONNET I, 137 (178)

The morning come, they
breakfast together.
For the new year
they are tolerant.
I thought
these were perilous times.
I parted
with these words
as we joined hands
upon the ground.
For all the way
is full of crags.
And spattered upon the rock
he went down.

SONNET II, 217 (239)

The day dawned, and held
and oh, joy!
appeared no more.
These graves
lie heaped
with stones.
The traces
slowly blotted.
The sun set,
forsaken.
We descended.
Beyond
a napping gazelle
answered.

SONNET I, 383 (429)

A billow
stiffened
upon the valley wall.
In the dusk
seek comfort
in the sand
and lay down suffering
with a kind inquietude.
I slept
till the autumn.
In the last weeks
I had
I thought I would
I breathe again.

Inherit.

SONNET I, 444 (491)

They see a stranger,
a banished man,
exile,
go home to his house.
The charitable call him
an unhappy fugitive, not an excommunicated person.
His fault is human and not divine.
No danger, I think.
I fell asleep.
They roused me.
Simple sayings
set
with my frank word of denial.
They said.

SONNET II, 444 (474)

They are mostly
at home
I cannot ride.
Stay
in the field.
We have two.
Who was with them?
Many.
I heard this parley in the garden.
Follow.
They are well
in the way.
They will bring back the
old and upward.

SONNET II, 237 (259)

Of human hypocrisy
there is no second giving.
We bless the man.
We drink and return.
We rose to depart.
He gently delayed us.
The second spring-time
flowed
and I saw
this new sweet
memorial.
Gentle entertainment
full of
fear.

SONNET I, 176 (218)

The weak must bear
and the poor
have all the blame.
He understood that
men
came.
Truth,
this honest opinion,
has
turned.
Night
be known.
Such losses happen every year,
not some.

SONNET I, 351 (396)

Speak
in the matter,
in the succulent spring
the great unwieldy brutes rise.
It happened then.
A pity
ought to have been observed.
Fortune had given us both
since the hope
failed
in his heart,
had not deceived him,
had not intended,
would not have.

SONNET II, 266 (290)

I knew certain
this could not help.
It was evening, and now we went.
The sun was setting
between.
When we came to them the young
fall stiffly
upon
their knees.
They lie still
till the morning.
It
thundered.
We went apart.

SONNET II, 127 (146)

He was pleased, but could not easily follow
since the whole world is flat.
Thou art a magician.
Save the deaths of some
of my labour.
Read in them all
the ears of the respectable.
Morning
waiting.
There might be
the truth.
But I must
lay a blame upon
him.

SONNET II, 9 (23)

He could guess
if any mocked, with great bursting forth of
furious eyes.
His long sufferance of the malice of the world might be this
resolution in him, to safeguard another.
As I returned
I met
company
in the fields.
I sat down
all round the sheet, but rarely fell within it.
He was amongst them
looking through spectacles
with the love of novelty which is natural.

SONNET II, 282 (306)

Before us
a flat mountain.
We went
under
a rocky passage.
But I heard.
The country was left empty.
Nothing is seen beyond
a desert world of new
mountains
and a
wilderness.
He bore upon his shoulder
magnanimous utterance.

SONNET I, 399 (445)

Fail.
This is a neighbourly custom
easily received.
Knit again.
After long indulgent amity
several interests are touched.
Brawls happen all day.
The policy of
lying together.
Approach and sit round.
Though it be a poor mess
his heart
is there to serve
a good while.

SONNET II, 61 (77)

One morning
with a loud good humour he praised the
company.
But the sun suddenly set
quaking
at a distance
under the cliffs

I saw
the shadows
running down.
Black domes
everywhere.
I asked my companions
coughing and laughing.

SONNET II, 236 (258)

We lay down.
An hour or two later this generous
steaming mutton heaped upon it.
A little milk spilled
out of countenance.
May the Lord give thee life.
But first
they have kept back nothing.
He holds his hand still,
rises and
puts the hungry
out of countenance.
Their fingers are expert
in all their deeds.

REPORT TO THE WORKING PARTY. ASYLUM. OTIOSE

(1979, Revised)

PACKING

The corn snow breaks its mass
under the shovel. It dries out
where it is least expected. I
gain an idea of greater mass.

Will you send it packing or heap
it on this side of the gravel
where rivulets drain away under-
ground.

You cannot see the rivulets but
the incisions, the bedding drifts,
expose their run.

PAPER

Paper slips from a machine. We
cut the ragged edge to usable size.

Ready discoloration replaces the
bleach and the pulp is undamaged.

CONE

There are spruce, fir and pine.

COLLISION

Technically
I stop there.

AY

Poor you.

You are not Russian
like this.

You pace about.

Your shuffle steps.

HOT

I cannot get
it down.

The head splits.
Leavening.

It gels.

NITROGEN NARCOSIS

I bury my head
deeply.

I am occupied.

I have no
stomach.

I stay.

WINDOW OF AIR

I no longer
define
an approaching motor

in the city evening.

Refraction.

I was driven away.

A window of air appeared
before me.

Widower I said.

There was no answer.

I went away
from this correlation.

PROTESTATION

This development
numbs.

I am hardly
at peace.

I behave thus,
feel this

orbital strain.

EAST

A static light
across the shut eyes,

inordinate forehead.

LOOKING AROUND

We hold under
the sweatiness.

I have infinite patience
watching them eat and sit
their papers.

HISTORY

How does one raise a finger
to save a suicide.

PINES

I hear what you tell me.

I ask a little.

Sorry is not sorrow.

The many-specied violet
blooms.

The road cambers.

Larch.

I AND THEY IN DISAGREEMENT

Here, living amongst the
normal and the un-
normal, I begin to shake my head.

I kick.

I invent despairing gestures.

YOU AND I IN AGREEMENT

Devotion places these hands
in our body.

LEDGE

This is, perhaps, where
a level of learning defeats.
Now led, now lead. Edge.
This language is so near,
on edge, must escape.

Scarf skin now litters the paper,
as it were a plane.

PSYCHOLOGICAL MOBBING

Waiting to be seduced
by the portent,
Aryan run dry,
has no validity.

Here, then, as the frailty
of human expression,
is that healthy disregard,

trying to live another day
without expenses

certainly, without understanding.

CANCELLED

Your books are all very nice.

I imagine them my own, for a moment.

What I am thinking about is not to be found
in any of its transmigrations or particles.

Virgin's bower is sometimes traveller's joy.

Your smile is radiant.

STRINGS

Dipping into the ink
we have survived the experience—
we survive the experience
resting our love in a sling or two,

an instrument to piece together,

we dream duets.

MALADJUST

These are small advances
made against deep hurt.

BEFORE LANGUAGE

I cannot sleep.

I walk about.

I leaf through several books.

I write.

LEVEL

I cannot get rid of this I.

INTONATION

My sight is held by you, kindly.

Let us suppose kindness,

Remissive to think *just* of the ground.

And what is wrong with this national inevitability.

Everything!

MUSICAL CHAIRS

How easy to operate on the assumption,
an historic assumption
that we inhabit the world,
our own a(e)ffront(ery).

With such limited resources
we turn and return.

We are made aware of that necessity
of unveiling refrains.

SNYFLUNG

The wretch goes to bed,
excruciating social disorder.

Appropriate music.

We waited for tomorrow
sorrowfully.

But that is all over.

White titters, and black titters.

Tomorrow, like today.

All unwretched.

Nice titties.

THY DÆMON

I remember my past.

And bits of conversations.

BENEDICTE

I hope you have a good Easter also.

PARTING OF THE WAYS

FRAGMENT I

Almost asleep, over this paper,
seeing the sun's shadow pointing out the stone
     boundaries of hill pasture,

FRAGMENT II

I wake up in a stone farmhouse.
The sun is up.

In the evening the scent of the stock, gilliflower,
     through the open window.

FRAGMENT III

—

COMPLAINT

I am not fat,
how could you say that.

And my skin,
should it be so thin.

Would it be better
if you were fatter and thicker.

Or if I should love you
with a kid glove.

CLAIM SONG

Tisane Tzigane

Hang the mirror
buy some tea.
Kiss your father
now kiss me.

Hang the mirror
stew the tea.
Kiss your mother
now kiss me.

Hang the mirror
pour the tea.
Kiss your brother
now kiss me.

Hang the mirror
drink some tea.
Kiss another
now kiss me.

REMONSTRATE

I am beautiful in my body
weak in my body.

You turn against me
by day.

And you are fitful
by night.

DEAD

A chameleon
(it had been butterfly before) inside you died.
It had been so green.

Butterfly caught in filigree
in dream. It had pale wings.

SPEAKING

I don't understand
this part, and that's it.

Disaffectionately,
say it were the age
were it not also your sister's manner.

THE UNPARDONABLE

It seems
as if I have done the unpardonable.

By not abandoning this friend, also artist,
or wrongfully interpreting this deeper spirit,
I intrude upon the peace of lovers.

Having no peace.

TARGET

You were not kind.

It is not true
that I hate.

I watched you throw aside root
or fly.

It's nothing.

Why do you hate?

Suck me,
as you like.

Spit it out.

NOT GODLIKE

No

    —

the poet is not god

    you know this

and since god was not there
    say the poet is

as ordinary as you are

    sanguine, fearful and un-

loved,

    you know this.

THE ARDUOUS MEADOW

The girls look like Alices

so one's own life is possible
beyond Fiddler's Green.

Is it imaginary?

What are their lives like
at such a distance?

He is walking, like a wise parent,

with his daughter.

THE ALMOND

Today is a bad day—
Before you went away.

I consult the same clock—
And you wear your white frock.

I have that much to fear—
By which you disappear.

Your imposed widowhood—
I have not understood.

[Your imposed womanhood.]

I see you standing where
the terrain dupes your care.

　　And your pallid stone
irretrievably stone.

The memory of my
insensitivity

buries you beneath the
dry track of my skis.

.

You are still—like the pine.
You tremble with the birch.

You go to earth, bitch fox.
But the cold drives you out

into the secrecy
　　of sophistry.

THE SEVENTEENTH OF MAY

Art has not made our life
but it provides a shift

of unacceptable
truths derived from trouble.

An example: how touched
on tragedy and vouched

for by such behaviour,
unexplained, and referred

to the authorities.
Suddenly, the police.

FROZEN

I would like to walk over
again the city river

not alone, as I write this,
but quietly, with you, the least

revered of my rational
dreams. Oh yes, a miracle.

TRAUMA

Why should I be here? And
what should I do? Friendless

irritably stateless.

TRACK

O categoric presence,
just pretence.

ENTROPY

I do not forget.

I risk this defense
in my left hand brain and my right hand.

Speak to me!

Implore *me* to come back to *you*.

PASS

And why, beneath the shade of this lamp,
why are you so sad?
And if I am it is because I
have lost my head.

It was Christmas Eve and your birthday
with fjord and spruce.
That was your home and you heard the way
you were spoken to.

TURN

It is only now after so many months
that I have begun to realize
your full force.

INDISTINCT VOICES

Where does the distinction end?
The vodka helps me feel my
home, a fragile handicap.
There you attack the keyboard, fend
off foes with gamey strength. I
cannot help you but I clap.

POEM

No.

QUEST

That was an accident.
In dreams responsibilities begin,
interrupted by a cat's meow.
And where did that come from?
Whatever we have meant,
to each other, with repeated words, and in
dreams, singular and repeated, how
shall we know this is home.

PSALM

Day unto day
speech.

Night unto night
knowledge.

PLANETS

–
–

–
–

   affections and afflictions
–

YOU BREAK

I made a mistake.

I do not want you to come to nothing
but you do not let me

want.

COME

You do not come.

I would like you to come.

You said you would come.

You said now you would never come.

VEIFA

Wait. Not wait.

She is a waif.

JANUARY

What is credible?

I have said all this before.

Many things have lost meaning,
not everything.

TRUE MEANING

What do you insist on?

Reasons, reasons.

Incisions.

Whatever happened,
this is my true meaning.

ENDANGERED SPECIES

I have almost nothing to say.

185

SPIRIT IS RENEWED

Baste the bird. Placate
live coals. Depend on it
for misery. Or mimic
the dark plaits that twilight
secularly highlights.

FELL

I know that voice, tiny
in love. Try to rest.

We are not connected.
Now you are their guest,

and they are concerned at
the hotel, distressed.

And up in the mountains
the theatre sets.

REFUSAL TO KNOW MORE THAN YOU

It is not known

if it were true suffering

who you were.

YOU

You would like to go back
to Russia

because clarity
has nothing to do with

your heart
or happiness.

LIFE, LOSS

There is a misreading.

MOVEMENT

We go.

Clearly.

It was possible to say so.

DECISIVE

The crack of dawn appears as a false seer.

COMMITTED

Flowers are blossoming

Birds are singing

Glass is lying on its side

SHAM

You think you are safe there.

You think you are safe now.

RANDOM

This is what I see—

IMPERFECT FAITH

You lie in the water.

You are so perfect.

You are so quiet.

In the water you glisten.

You glisten in the water.

I disturb you with the tips of my fingers.

A film of liquid unites your edges and bursts
because I lift you from the water.

I lift you from the water.

I quickly restore you.
You are perfect.

You are still.

THE EDGE OF THE LAND

Even when it is dull
there is a light from the water

which loosens me
which lightens me.

It does not matter whether it is light from a fjord
or a lake

or light from the sea which is always thinking about
whether to abolish the edge of the land.

WEIGHTS

We are built differently.

And is this the reason?

As pragmatic as the shape of anchors.

YOUR AMBITION

You have what you want.

Have I?

I BEGAN

I misled myself and I was misled as
if by the lighthouse that no longer
guided the ships safely clear of the
shoals because of the silting up of
the point.

WITH YOUR BROADNESS AND YOUR TIGHTNESS

I remember you as mushrooms.

DARKNESS

I will let you go
because you no longer implore me.

CONSEQUENCES

The balance in things in you and me
is disturbed.
It is like writing with the unfamiliar
lightness of a pen without its removable cap.
It is like drumming with lightweight sticks.

YOUR DEMAND

I see my country
—which is my country?
not knowing what to do
—what should we do?
I see myself
—and who is that if not you?
not knowing what to do
—what then should I do?

I should listen to your deepest secret.
I should watch with your sharp and wondrous eyes.

And what I learn I should not turn inside out
and against you.

I BELIEVE YOU

I turn out the light
and turn to the wall.

I am worn out.
I am warm here.

I will address myself to you.
I will disappear with my mistake
and you with yours.

CLARITY

I turn the light towards me.

It is an old desk lamp
with slack springs
and an overheated shade.

It stands on a small worn table
together with a typewriter
a lantern and candle
a telephone
some books and papers
a watch
a pipe
pencils
cigarettes and matches
a drawing pin.

FAR

You draw aside the curtain.

The window is not clear.

You no longer know what you are saying.
You no longer know what to say.

You know your life will be difficult
though once you thought otherwise.

THE LETTER

It is no fault of ours that we do not agree
but we were interrupted
and did not know how to resist.

I ASSURE YOU

If you think
there are moments which are spurious
you are mistaken.

YOU SEE THROUGH ME

I see myself through you
but not in you.

I see you also.

PHRASAL

I turn away from you
whom I no longer know.

I turn towards you
whom I do not know.

We were gentle.

You were one and the same.

POSITIONING

Placing a cushion beneath you
or at you makes all the difference to you.

CADENCE

I cannot describe the colour
of the flowers I give you.

PEACE

This scene is pastoral.

A flock of sheep grazing
in the meadow

as an ornament.

And the daffodils beneath the trees.

RUINS

I follow the way the river bends.
I follow its bank
against the current.

CATASTROPHIC

We drove out.
I think of a troika

or a droshky.

In the eye of the snow
we were driven out.

POWERLESS

I am held by my wrist.

NEITHER TO DISPARAGE NOR FLATTER YOU

The snow flakes into the water
and the oil flows off shore.

What conditions!

I trace a thin colourless line
where your lips might be.

Your hat and your coat.

I regale you with words
whose powerlessness gladdens me

with words which do not portray you.

HOMMAGE NUL

You are neither the unnamable nor the unspeakable.

CRISIS

Snows or dunes.

PENITENT

Look, I shall look upon you
no longer
or for as long as I want.

I shall turn you into
a kind of stone—

Quicker than you turn me
into a kind of harness.

Horse, water.

Your soul is a pool
and you will lie in it
in all weathers,
a kind of stone.

Though you welcome the water
you will be rheumatic

yet with dryness you will become parched.

Gentle or apprehensive
you will touch your throat

and call to me.

AT NIGHT

I cannot sleep.

I hear talking
and the slamming of doors.

ATROCITIES

Films are made of massacres.

Filming massacres
is not enough.

Whether making or filming occurs first
and is wilful.

WAVES

I see the way
you are suspicious
and hide her.

ANIMATE

Because your hand is not here
I rest my brow
against the cold frame of a desk lamp
and my hand against the heat of its shade
where your breast might be.

AS THE LIGHT, SO THE COLD

Lengthens,

Strengthens.

It should have gathered us.

First light deified us.

Because I cannot talk to you.
Because you will not let me.

Alleviate our suffering and bad dreams.

Why.

Encompassed.

Our lips should be sacred.

Scarred

and defied.

XV SECTIONS

I

Will you kiss my sweetness?

No, no, how it breaks off
in the company of your beautiful life.

Leaves a trace, a little grit
gone for a walk in the mountains.

Weigh, weigh.

II

You can.

III

You've done it now.

I won't tire myself out
in that mad city
where the exhaust is enclosed
and the cunt slop doused.

You won't be a great painter.
You aren't willing to suffer.

IV

We are pushed.

I am the latest last romantic,
I travel, I travel.

V

The chatter, chatter
the play.

Are you good to me? Mist.
We all think it's a good idea.

Allowed to wander Professor
between the lakes
only with a sense of loss.

O surreptitious splendours,
if you only knew.

VI

Y quién clama las doce no son trece.

And you understand
on this snow swept plateau
full bin of rubbish
how she hates you and all think
you will kill her thus thou she

Anaemic remorse.

My love is vapour.

211

VII

Your hands are beautiful!

Quietly.
I feeel them.

I shall beauty you with my hands.

What's to be done with loneliness
except to cry,
or not to.

What have you dreamt since then
since the clucking hen
en
de d.

VIII

Does the whole world revolve around
love?

My beautiful woman.

The Lord Mayor
has no hair.

Your hair is washed
forever shiny, soft
and curlicues.

Scratch your little parasites
your little mites.

What a beauty. That I have.

IX

In doubt I trust.
This angular flower
picked for you wants to speak.
And please let it.
Pink, white it doesn't matter,
only take care, dear one,
what a hard, harsh course
without retribution
as I don't know you will.

X

I love your stocky,
your high cheekbones,
dark, dark, red, red.

My veins are swollen,
you lift your racket
and storm. I love your thighs
I see up.

I would like to kiss you
and rub your pulled muscle.

XI

You and I stole circa 2000 kroner from I.

Who is I?

We surrounded the peak.
For the first time grow lemons, oranges
and a solitary grapefruit.

While painting a horrible man
touched your white, white thigh, he
doesn't mean to be horrible.

Horrible, horrible, horrible.

All the horrible things you can think of.

Dream, dream, tell me it is a dream.

XII

If you saw me now
like this with a mask
of whitened beard.

Occasional strands
enveloping

my true magnetic

sneeze.

XIII

Nought now inspires.

What's to be done?

Don't wait but
get on.

Why worry for the paper pieces
and skeleton leaves.

They've exposed you
but those who don't.

XIV

Conical rosewood

whatever wood you are
I put you to my lips.

Listen, shawn trumpet.

There is no doubt I saw you there.

Was it miserable to hide
your white smock
below the graeness
of your lover's lap
his shitty pants.

XV

I don't hold a red candle up to you.

Not up to your face.

But I won't live any uncomfortable lie.

Leave it unsaid. Don't say anything to anybody.
Isn't that right?

And lift up your legs. Kiss
each other's feet soles.
Let us crush new fallen snow
to our rosemaling cheeks.

SEEDPORT

The effects
do not match the images.

Think of stars
how they twinkle.

Love is sweet
oh bitter sweet.

Damp damp
springs to life
o'er ' land.

When winter winds blue o'er ' land.

Then I wrote about
paths

and I am happy
though alone
though I do not think I am happy

though nervous.

Do not be so.

If only
if only.

A lady bird
alights on the tube.

A whole herring
follows tail.

In the wall's shade.

Look at leaf.

Closely.

Imperfect ivy leaf.

Found in the hill.

No in.

A lane on the hill.

I am for life.

Bas showing
a musician.

Bas on base.

Bass.

Reorder the room.

Compel. You compel
yourself.

Disorder.

Forget language
forget feeling
remember anything
foresee
tell

hearing

relief

obverse.

Bombs and fires
gave them the chance.

Siberian wastes
gave us the chance.

The impression went
leaving pains.

223

At the back of the throat
the knife.

At the blade of the throat.

There was nothing surreal
about it, everything sure.

Where boats go in and made
for the open sea.

This is how things happen.

Fractions. Eying
the distance between shoots.
They meet at the signal box
in a summer fragrance.
The sleepers go on, and something
disappears into the bank.

Along the edge of hedgerows.

Butterflies.

A light haze.

Strains.

'I haven't the least idea.' Nor I.
   My old pupils move to the rocks
in a westward way. They
   stare at the poplars bordering
France along the head. A
   swelling on your lower lip.
You are bruised. You don't like it
   one bit. Close ranks.

You do not believe
in gold miracles.

May floods
flooded the autumn
meadows.

These boats were
rowed.

A view of the world—

frightened you
of and after this.

The wind stops
with you.

What is yes what is
the point of this

grease dirtying
the trouser leg
you were so careful.

What can you do
when peace is disturbed
and the game is seen
for the game

when the wind stops
without you.

Do these lines ever meet.

When hurriedly you put down the book
some pages crease.

And begin
towards such a meeting.

Where your eyes rest.

An aeolian scarecrow
flashes the yellow mustard fields.

Your eyes rest
against black fields.

Earth dried out
with the wind beginning
with the sun beginning.

A fledgling swoops
over seedport.

Lightning and thunder.

Like the kestral, cloud-men
perform before the day is gone.

Between the alveoli
of high & low, the sun shone.

How will you know when the water tower
shall be filled when you cannot see over
the edge.

How shall you know when the resting bell
will sound when you cannot cannot will
it.

Oars,
you are rowing
the stream.

There
there is overhang
of willows, willows.

Here
here is flotilla
of leaves, leaves.

Mothers and Fathers—
—knew fear
and we rowed far, far.

Oars,
you are rowing.

Lace-edged,
frilling
as in is a provider of thrills.
Lace-edged
rhizomes where the cloth
presses in folds in the leg
by the stool leg
sketched in.
A trill of a rhyme.

Naked
in long grasses
and bedstraw
grows bodily in the way
of the chattering children.
The path you take
the path we take
the path they take.
There a wood bridge
was here mold beams are.

Naked
in long grass
and bedstraw
the body grows in the way
of chattering children.

Path worn to mud. Fish arise.

The fish coughs.

No it is a human.

The sun and the straw.

Solarizes.

The wards of society.

The fish is double.

No one is here now.

One day the sun shone
a strong wind blew on the second
and so on—

Will I ever stop thinking about you?

I expect the heron
to think about you.

I expect the heron
to conceal the hunt

far beyond the twentieth century

simulating flight.

To write down what you hear
to answer what you are asked
to close the gap between differences

in a corner quiet
half in the shade
near the pigeons

a word
not yet identified
watches over you.

Mother of eye
I see you in
the rose
of the painting
of your self-portrait.

I am there too
sniffing oysters.

Petals fall
past life.

Some things
turn into you.

Things living beyond
their meaning.

If so unwise you are, or
so unhappy as to miss, oh dear

the way to build worlds.

I remember the wind—
why! it is here now.

I heard this
far

I do not speak of it.

BLUES THAT MUST NOT TRY TO IMITATE THE SKY

(1978)

No blue is crossed out
and you would not do not for your speed of writing
is drawn busily across the washing line.
And on the reverse no it is not the reverse
but another sheet the washing is crazy in the sun and wind
spreading across Bastia. I am your suitor
and we show affection, sometimes
it is great sometimes it is in the most unlikely or likely
of places where almost everything is shared
and everything eventually. Crithmum maritimum grew out of the rocks.

You were not trying to drag anybody into the gutter,
I know that and my words were wrong and you were right
in that spontaneity which it triggered
leaving you by the quay and me in the rue
de l'Opera. I walked slowly away and you drank a whisky
I expect.

Determined to make this long
enchanting you, everlasting my love
revealed and you still find you
can breathe like me. I find that
too. Parts of the past are not easy.
Or the present even, as when the tractor grows
aware of us pitching our love
on the lovely part of that bank of meadow
bruising the umbellifers blistering
the skin my love.

It is evening. The labiates spread
here beside the stony bed of the river.
The leaf is so gentle. As a plunge washing the sweat and dirt.

When I see you I want to kiss
you so much that it is so simple,
I set out walking I felt like John Clare
I passed hens pecking at the black nuts of persicaria.

Feeling as if you had recognized
something akin to what is
recognized in you.

The story is wrong. Lies
were told and therefor' intended.
Polygamic, but admiring. The

colour of the sky changed: strong, strange;
weak, warm; later uniformed
indifference glossed as friendship.

Blake or Yeats slept with you nervously
wrecked but
tired and departed.

This may change.
                    If not
it is a dying race against
guillotines, a late

gittern, computing to *home*.
The colours change,
accompanyment is out, the knuckles

bare in the hills, is this
denied? Only, you, may, write
well.

Your striking hand *is* life
& death. Fidelity is expended, not dog-like.
And the kitten plays with the mouse.

QUIET FACTS

(1979)

—

1

The burn from the glowing
element
on the finger.

The shadow of the hand
out of the corner of the eye.

Untitled.

2

The gathering of dust.

The circle seared by a warm glass.

Oppressed head.

A grey sock belonging to you
who are not here.

3

Cat and kitten.
What is one and what the other?

They are first together
and then separated.

Their image dependent.

4

Inside

the wind is stuck.

The cobweb.

Here at the altar.

The Corsican pine.

And something we understand

more than wild.

5

The wind is stuck here.

Axe and axle.

The eye lash.

The pared nail.

Broken moons.

Gun shots from the dead hunter
raising new squeals.

6

Peg of drift wood.

Sandalwood.

Salt.

You.

Trembling.

Infinitely beautiful.

7

The eye clouds.

Or the lens.

The bank of cloud moves heavily,
quickly.

The gull.

The sentiment.

8

Mica.

The speakers either side, on either side.

Slats.

Sadat.

Jerusalem.

Biko.

Sadat.

Jerusalem.

Biko.

Jerusalem.

Biko.

9

You
tremble for another.

For a moment, and
for another moment.

We know and we understand
without knowing the burden.

We say you are a friend
who understands.

10

When the pipes enter
the iron stove.

Then, the diamonds
cut across everything.

We do not live here for ever.

Diamonds of twigs
diamonds of stone
diamonds of air.

11

We let the water stagnate.

So the stalks dry.

They symbolize what is common,
like coins.

12

What is poetry?

I do not know.

13

The curves,
the occurrences.

They do not harden for us.

The wind rips the branches.

Sighs, and sighs

turning into mother blackbirds.

14

The rain brings down.

After rain
is when the skies become
heavenly.

Then we can decide whether
to talk about heaven and earth
or sky and earth.

In that way we would like
to be overwhelmed.

15

The bovine horn
has one note.

Glacial plains
on the surface.

So the note carries.

Towards the edge of the world
appear cracks.

16

Burning ears
burning eyes
burning brow

peaceful and excitable.

The thumb pinched
where it is bleeding under the sun.

What are you thinking
what are you doing now

with your taut and lovely fingers
radiating strings
radiating holes
radiating pictures

radiating

17

The music
describes an arc

but not only an arc.

I look to where
you are open with a third eye.

I hear you say
'Come and be happy in my room'.

18

The house at odds.

We both came out of this same
house at odds.

19

Gentle phases of the moon
and tides.

20

In the night,
with your blue eyes,
skidding at the edge of ploughed fields,
wheat like you.

Orbiting.

A WHITE MESS

(1981)

In the revolutionary shout
is the shoot
burning in her garden
under summer skies.

In March you greeted me
with raised eyes and
fanned tail.

Soon you sang often.

As I leave the house
your eye follows me, drives out,
and eyes me closely
from the fence as I pause
an eye-draught through the window.

I was bewildered
and did not stand
at the appointed place.

I wonder at what
has become
this water
flowing into oblivion.

This clear circular oblivion.

I see, in the light
of the following year
what is now.

Nature has freed me
in touching me with thorn
straw, sting and myriads
of things.

But I cannot go outside
this Nature.

So late the year
the flowers open

the tree curves in blue space.

And leans over the worker.

The blue
now incandescent
I cannot see at the moment
(was it green)
62½ plus or minus 2
(I went blind) horizons screen
(they are blue).
But over the horizon
falling snow,
and beyond the horizon
fallen snow
and nowhere the light of your upward glance
and nowhere petulance.

My voice nothing to you
but a perfect *Digitalis purpurea.*

THE PIPE ORGAN BUILDERS

With my ears and my eyes

There was a dream
that you called out
that you called out

There was no rest
under the eiderdown

There was the smell

There was the forgotten dream
because I did not write it down
when I awoke

You lit the night light

You remembered your forefathers

And why were you alone

You did not understand

The light flickering on the ceiling

At this peace

This house

Where the water boiled

The smoke was a swallow

The brook reflected

Shooting stars

Exfoliation

The wood

The smoke

The bronze instrument

The cold clear policies

It rests in the palm
lining up as the register
of a graph of white bands,
it's hard to say how they
got there, the trajectory
arrives at the summit
splashed out a bit, where
have I seen something like
this before, a nebulae,
like any other, it might be
a map of the world or the
universe, microcosm of it,
I rather think it's something
more mundane, sparkling a
little.

Autumn
carries the unfulfilled past
of tragedies

There, was a poor, bare, peg doll,
lying in the earth.
Her flush changed to a dry, dull
sadness. She
went to school feeling good
under her skirt

A sweep of the hand
brushed the crumbs off the table
and the fingers caught the book
spinning it off the edge
and the world *here* was flat
straightening like starting

Stone

In the wind, the gate
an animal

The sky clear blue

Smoke

Eyetricks

The turbulent flow
of the footpath

a night of shivering
a night of heaviness

The lights of the workshop
made eight coffins

The shadows of the branches
through the windows

Swirling

Waiting

The diplomat

Every word belongs
to another

Every bird

It stays in the memory

This leaf is a map of the world
and it is flat

There is a suspicion

This leaf is about the size of an oval coin

Yellow

Neither graceful
nor sand

Stone rings
from whence

it was first active
then static

it turned to stone
unsure of its standing

Each day brought a new
tribulation

a red glow in the night sky

The stone curled its rings
its rings

A gentle voice

even

even

The stream led into a river

I stood by the grave memorials
in stone

The pipe organ builders
were trying to play two notes
the second fractionally before
the first

The red door

The far red illumination

The heat made it difficult to breathe

Are these wings or are these shells
is this cake or is this real

I woke to the sound of bells
and rose again
and rose again
for these wings or these shells
these cakes or these reels

Cramp seized me
as I knelt

What goes on?

Inveterate construct

We were playing something else

273

Morning

I am blessed with light

The Romans
left
of

I do not say they should
they did not

past this stone

You see the Saxon angled stone
said
said

If you do not lie
you have no imagination

And
this may be true
where

Scattered

You
imagine what happens

but cannot

The Lakes

I am here
and you also
returning
in the formal streets
of the gas lamps
and the shapes I see appearing
appear to me
as a spectre

You disclaimed
the punctuation mark
in the silence
I heard
above the din
I felt the change
and unsettlement
of these shifting, refracting
lines

Some words
took shape
across the plane

These Glyphs
cut across
where ash burgeons
the plane

What do you think of me
of course, I wonder and I care,
if I could take this risk
and what it means
to understand the loving
one the weakness

and you not miracle

I felt this chill
and the irritation in my nose
and the smoke lying

nowhere else

I cannot answer this

I cannot answer

now

it was new
made for you

Those unforgettable opportunities

it was old
fashioned in gold

I stepped off on to rock
where it was

The triumphant turn
of the orchis

There came over

The bud was exposed

I was

The rest was

Long golden flashes

And now the sun is out
the day spreads through
the open window

Shapes and hues

The secret began

Invisible words

Glowing with heat
Glowing with suck

Quivering

Somewhere a shutter closed

A sudden change
came over the stone mist
sprigs of lamb
twists and turns
rang the moon
over the stone
and the lights travelling
beside the lake

Roared the gas lamp
as the gas grew light

The small white room
watched its brown ceiling
curving towards it

Orange flares
made extraordinary greetings

The Sea

On the beach
the tree
just

fell

The dominant politics is this

Nuclear power is crude

Nuclear power is degenerate

Along the shore
the rippling of the water
glazes over the stones'
weeds

The wind blows
my innocence
my ignorance

The sea is like a great gong

Thickly

Memorable
memory
memorial

What happens

changes into script

Awoke
before the flood

Firm
and consequent

Said
always come back to
what you wish you were

A carpet of flowers

The sky delivering itself

We are black
and do not know it

o wheel, ᴏ ball

was he king
of the myth
was he fisherman
was he blind
was he mineral
was he silent
was he dead
in this North Sea
in this old sea

It took days to recover
inexplicable day

Inexplicable daze

Work

that disappears

holds the clue

There are no genetically stable
types

I came here like anyone else

The play came to me in a dream

He disappeared
inside himself

God
the self

could not go any further

A voice said throw off Greece

War prides

Drops

for F A

Holds the (ᴗ)

Of colour

Of water

That works

That vaults

—

Love
can be

almond eyes

thick lips

hips

wiry hair

and the jaw

of any

number

of lost

tribes

MOVING BUILDINGS

(1982)

I left the sun
striking my eyes

*

The romance is not lost

The buds
awoke

This simple statement
of the facts

*

Lives you do not see through

*

My manor is not my manor

*

There is a glance between
the sun and rain

April
loses me
above the small trees of April

*

There is a world between *I wish
I was* and *were*

I was is really here
but *were* not there

*

In each passing second
of the sun's rays

*

And behind the old manor
where I sought

the white and sand butterfly

O Provençal spring

I found

the little doves

and all manner of pornographic life
discarded

in the strange, unimaginable
curve

There was moss
where the water ran

You carried yourself
gently

You sat on the rocks
by the river
stripping bark off

where stones get holes
get flutes

where little birds
were singing in the night

of shining Provence light
on stone and head
when rain stops
in months of April
May

and none stops
at the narrow gap of
winding gates in
winding gates

then sometimes something happens

*

Many blues, many hours

Life has not been very clear
here oh why, I know, don't
know, not finding some little
homes, least, not a recognition,
homes of elegance like
emptiness. Not wide
empty spaces—faces of the
gestures move, oh yes,
that move

It gets
bigger and bigger

miracle corrupt

the mineral frame
is not seen when it goes
under

Inclined the head too much
but upright

I said
this conglomerate is not right
and ends a few years hence

No idle threats of idle works

There is a loss
on this pointlessness

Some lovely girl woman

silent in waves

who might be
Soviet

yet settles
in the country of their forebears

*

Vietnamese forbearers

This clue
is the surface

some floating liquid

escapes

a variable number of
blue horizons

and one red and one

waving red

POLAND'S NEIGHBOURING COTTAGE

(1984-5)

Walking near
the house quite lost.

Carrying nothing.

Absence of ðī.

The snow driving there
and melting.

The scent of flowers.

Paradise.

A thousand lakes.

Round apples.

NORTH NORTH, I SAID, NO, WAIT A MINUTE, SOUTH, OH, I DON'T KNOW (148 POLITICAL POEMS)

(1985)

"The first of these was its high valuation of the idea of the answer in itself. For an answer is a rarer thing than is generally imagined.   There are many highly intelligent people who have no answer at all in them. A conversation or a correspondence with such persons is nothing but a double monologue—you may stroke them or you may strike them, you will get no more echo from them than from a block of wood. And how, then, can you yourself go on speaking?"

"Nevertheless, we say, when a man has lost his memory, that he doesn't know who he is."

Takes
The edge away
from it.
As the edge
turns
at the edge
away from it.
Oh curious realm
wherein.

Flying
Away and
away
with the
rough and
unshaven appearance
swept by the winds
of the earth's
multiple appearances.

If
You wrote
all over
these mathematical
legends
you would be
reassured.

Flying
Through space
any awry space
whose true
name
as yet unknown
assumes
a three-way
plotting.

Smoke
And the sparrows
moving through the beads
of grass in time
to the overtures
of cork and sponge.

How
I longed for
the surrounding arms
to surround
you with
the thoughts
of flickering the light
and the shallows
of the leaves.

The
Truet
close to you
and still
closer
moving
over
unexpected
faults.

In
Resigning
from such effects
to what effect.
Effecting such
an unconvincing
resignation.

I
Turn
to leave
the space
of magical
worn and wary
encounters.

This
Will simply
surprise
the closest
overturning
inside the inferno
and upright
the proceedings.

And
Slowly
the wheel past.
What near
and clever
wishes
phased in
the eternal.

Different
Creatures weathering
the distances in
different ways.

Thrust
Upon one
unbelieving
breeze
firmer than ice.

        Sucked
By the lips
of the loving.
Amassed
by tongues.

        You
Do not come
out of this
densely packed mass
from where you were
scheduled. But
for what was
said again
this stubble
might take hold
of an imagination.

Practically
In this leaning
of and up against
a tree.

I
Was here
before.
I saw and
then forgot.

Changing
Voices changing
in the blind
ear. I try to forget
there was no mountain
here.

Empty
Phrases, lost applications,
past remedies.
Humectant sexuality.
Nubility in arms.

How
Has age
fitted you
for listening
to the past
once more in
the face of
the present.

        Silvery
Light on the
different species of tree
drawn through the
cloudy sky
changed the green.
If you do not know
what I write
or like
walk out into
the light,
there.

        An
Ancient play
often comes back
in the simple
confusion of
political
elegance.

You
Were dispossessed
by combats
close to the
zone
of the occupying
forces.

Crystal
Beyond yellow.
Token outrages.
We see
now
how one government
engineered
there be no war
whilst the other
engineered
the war
as the first
knowledgeable
condition.

When
I wanted us
to meet I did not
want to move
more than half
way.

More
Than once
I felt close
to the discovery
but I did not
appreciate
how these things
were done.

Not
To call up
the demons
who imitate you.
Not to travel
distances
where you get nowhere.
Or remain
in a place
where you are given
to feel
or at least feel
you are
somewhere.

Which
Fence face fire
will be what
you wanted
and did not
appreciate
enough
on the day
it passed
halting.

You
Draw things
into you.

Lost
Face awaiting
nothing yet
attending
everything.
Placated
image of the
world.

Half
Ambition
foraging in
the cities
and provinces
even those
named
beautiful
for the self
feeling
spinning
with promises.

Poised
For what incredible angles.
Flight designing
different destinations
with nothing clear
above the clouds.

A
Plantation
of tiny wild
strawberries
wildly affected
by the few
passes there.

In
The settlement
of unchartered difficulties
a town
blots out the earth
blots the word
blots the use it pays
for at the touch of
murderous vaults and in the
present adoration of the
war.

     But
Somewhere there
plastered on to
the walls I dream
the dream of
scandals and
ordinant flesh.

     I
Raise myself
into these mountains
uneasily
existing here. I call
to the legendary spirits
left behind in the far north
in which naturally
I reluctantly
believe but
nevertheless believe
in order to remain.

Not
To examine
closely
the tears of pride
restoring me
to the knowledge
of all humanity.

Broad
Scapes from everything
to nothing
and back to
everything again.
Bound and released
the moving plant
elevates there
in the forest
and defies
the keeper.

    Not
To avoid the
deflection into
the aesthetic
arch. Alive
to each moment
railing against
the whole lyric
purpose in trying
to establish the
meaning of
the wasting
of time.

    You
Know I cannot
easily
deal with
that purposeful
ambition towards
mediocrity. So
clear to see,
so clear it
cannot be
a matter to doubt.

When
Three dimensions
become as two
deceiving as a
card film set
you have
your photograph
printed in a book
and let your
reader question
what you want
with expressive
distractions
unlike any
record of
you at work.

Coming
Into algae
we do not
know how
this lets things
affect our
decisive desire.

When
The language
is stretched
to the last limit
of irreverences
then this is the time
when last needs turn
to latest and
through a few leaves
a last fruit
falls.

Light
Bursting
through cloud
as if mistakenly
mailing a letter
in a litter bin.

Suddenly
There is a seating
next to you
of great beauty
reflected through
the glass
like studied
attention
waking, walking
showery.

And
When the words
are spilt
like raffinose
I know it is
time to throw
it all away
for honey.

What
Lies between
the narrow
beams
depends
on conditions
of plight,
magnificence,
stacking and
proximity.

Practically
The only thing left
between the aerials
is the foundation
of the earth
and all the edifice
of the cobbles.

I
Cannot hide
behind what
I do or
disappear into
thick air.

Dispersed
Between the
leaves and
the realization
that some distractions
rise straight
from the stem
and warm embarrassed
feelings.

The
Crop spray chemical
is unquestionably safe. And we
know it to be patently
untrue, striking
the head
and the heart
stricken.

On
The condition
of slavery
beneath the sifting
salt
the drawn knot,
outrageous
suspicions
and teasel hostility
deny me
the riddle
of the mindless frame.

Do
People change—
Or Israel
what can I do
or refuse you
as easily as I do
my birth.

As
The others weave.
This edifice
alters the
exponential
relationships.
Purses the lips
at the remora
and appellation
of water. It is
a formidable
task.

No
Oceanic occasion
behind the false
beards, the hatches.
The under
the hatches implodes
into the name, ignorant,
so cluttered and clustered, it
means this.

You
Cannot recognize this
from such a distance
sounding far into the night
of the fornix.

The
Rock over
the cliff
over the sea
poised
and the prophecy.

The
Blue the
blue in the cloth,
to think
of this political
design,
or ignorant wearing
it, boring
into the cloth
refusing
the wrath.

Petals
Sprinkled
on the neglected
earth.

You
Lift the knee
of a stockinged
leg, the breast rose
beneath
and fell into
voices and cotton,
laps and hymns.

A
Walk through
the hills where
we is written
with a double
you.

It
Is easy
to stay here
beside the yellowing
ticket
and stones bridging
the water
and behold the
truth of those
fantasies
about which you
keep quiet and
in which you
are kept.

I
Hold an
unremitting emptiness.

Let
Inessentials pass. But
if they are essential
or essentials inessential
give the devil
his jeu.

You
Sense something wrong
and do not deny the sense
of what it is.

You
Press the
earth of
these images
here, and in
saying it
you think you
have an image
but
only the leaf
of an age.

The
Sudden change
of the weather
when travelling
or staying quiet—
warnings or no
warnings, but
now nowhere near where
is home for the
present, the silver
rains—yesterday
still, between the emblems
of the railings.

I
Do not want
to build
elements
of the tragic
or suffering
down.

Here
O Israel—
you are doing it here.
For all
pass over your rights
for all pass over
your safe conducts.
There is no doubt
you are quite
human
and henceforth
like anyone
else.

Cool
I was cool
as I never
was anywhere
except by the winter lakes
and summer lakes.
Spruce and fir
stepping down
there, reeds
improvising, the
unexpected
wave sounding.

Then
In naming
these arguments
stealthy with
the paws of
the shadow
furry with
the paws of
the shadow
of a leopard, then held
with the flow
of for and against.

I
Stayed to
watch the sun's
movement and
microscopic change.
I saw how
pure chance
explains
nothing at all.
I honour the
unexpected
calm I feel
rising
in me.

Look
For the pure
dreams of castles,
destroyed and
rebuilt as habitable
cottages, of forts
destroyed and
rebuilt as habitable
cabins.

When
My dear you are
covered with this
fur, this hair,
these feathers, this
miracle of
attachments,
this settling of the
emotions
is close.

The
Way you talk
and were reared
strains
the imagination
of loaded
condescension,
intonation of
the cynic.

. . . Like
Those gone
and those
to come, like
a tree, boleless.

Of
All that was
this and
was.

You
Know that
the wide harvester
has passed here
today harvesting
the boughs
hanging
over the road, the
world closely
devastated.

The
Table has dipped
from the pressure.
Heavy dictionaries
keeled into the dip.

The
Power of those
who have done
such damage
out of the
criminal light
shadowed over
by oblivion
predicated.

for Anne-Marie Albiach

The
Ages of reading the
grammar of
endless attachments
and disengagements.

Red
Blotches, rashes,
multiple wounds
brought to the
surface of the
skin, O light
so unbrilliant
on this second
day.

I
Drink stone-fruit
and dust.
I look
for figures
treading into the
wrong book.
I work
as an enemy.

Also
Now no
knowing what
she will do.
Sucker into
strange, sullen
looks.

These
Reproductions
these miniatures
these gratuitous
imperfections
wherein we live
in fake rigid
productions.
This o'clock feeling
for which you wouldn't
give the time
of day.

For
The bear
more than a century
passed in day
dreams and incubi.

Everything
You did not want
to hear, everything
you saw. The
silence you found
would stay with
you at dusk.

If
It is possible
survival depends
on some unimaginable
measure of attachment
to lakes, steppes,
fjell.

There
Are times
when the light
dimming lets us
see for example, a
reflected more
clearly.

Not
Yet lips of the world
—the image
covering up on
itself, talking
ways with a tongue's
charm.

The
Opaque language
of some books
does not exist.
There
is a closed
field, catching the
moment of a
gate latch.

Here
In the unspeakable
lesson the
rogue plantation
is piercing together
the poppies and
the oxeyes in a
dusty, peaceable
conception.

Waves
Of electronic
interference.
What good
is the wave
which seals
the fates of
everlasting
destruction.

New
Glue replaced
the damage
caught in the
net of the limbs.
This new
agony
of indecipherable
contra-
distinctions.

Statutory.
A heavy weariness
about so much
wearying, over
and over, the weary
utterances
lost for the moment,
lost for words.

I
Do not seem to know
how the world works.
And therein lies
the danger of in
action when all
weariness is not
yet at an end.

347

Sitting
Still above
water at the
cliff
cut
at the tree
crown you might
see or come
differently
to those things.

And
Finding
the empty envelope
between the
cover and
the paper
folded
twice
waiting
for the glyphs
to answer.

Through
Wrought iron
shelves disappear
and reappear.
Alarming
frequencies
of oceans without waves,
an image drinking
itself to death.

The
True critic
in the making
of a new work.
And the meaning
of all those great
collections of
the world.

Remembering
Where I had
never been.
Strange
homeliness of
a thousand unseen
lakes with
out mountains
or the idea
of its harrowed
memory.

They
Are the same
stars but
what if they
are.

A
Wishbone
far from everything
in the sky
leads me to
the image
of everything
there,
and these locks
exploding in the wishing
of imaginable
offspring.

In
The wide sweep
of the convoluted
drive I
round on the
scattered
pebbles.

Give
Me a landscape
containing me
however limitless
and limitlessly.
The one scattering
me in confusion
is above all fearful
even in its perpetual momentary
containment.

It
Is formulated
out of the bin
which is not
to say it
therefore becomes
beautiful
and.

In
Working to
relinquish
power I
cannot expect
to complain, whether
I do.

The
Sound carries
across this
expanse of
beach and sea
voices flying like
gulls and
broken resonances
fulfilling the promises
of broken shells
and silica.

Imperfect
As in the nature
of our appearances
and yet we work
to some notion
of perfect
refusing the
incompetence, some
of us,
and rightly so, of
the corrupt discourteousness
of cultural
slovens, who are
some of us, among
us scribblers, editors,
critics, lecturers, owners
of onus.

Because
I am the well-
spring, one of
many in many
trades and if
you do not believe
it put your lips or
the other way
and they will
I cannot be sure
honour the promise
they.

            Disturbed
By an inevitable
turbulence and the
sure knowledge
that certain
disturbances must
not be gainsaid
is a limiting
endurance. Vacant
scratchings at helpless
doors. Look, well
do not, if you insist
on the forceful exhibition
of this noise made
by a struck match you
pass over the choice
of utilizing such
strikes as survive
or some part
thereof. Truly, I
do not think of poetry
as any more or less
than that
movement. It
would be unreasonable
to suggest other
possibilities re
unreplenished drainage.

Storming
Inexpectant
so unexpectedly
with the news of
electronic
strafing. All
over now.

The
Metropolis
wants to suck
the work
into the media.

Whatever
Efficacy turns
to rock
or the rock
out of where
these classical
marble features
are both hidden
and hewn
and animated
in the language
of the next
seating cubicle.
There where and
here where some
gilding comes
to rest below
the ear.

Where
Shall I turn to
look to find
sweet words,
which deed
in my sack,
or should I
gare at rocks
and wooded walks,
stay behind at the
open gate.

357

        In
The evening
their definitions
crowd out for a stroll
from window to
window and the
ars poetica
conceives itself
as a judgment
on the specific
abstraction, here
called truth.
Then you come
to own what
you see other
matters.

        Smell
Of the Gymnosperm
inclined
hesitancy in the
bud
then bursting
segmenting.

        At
Rest like
a *Rubus arcticus*.

        Bit
Between the teeth
nearing the home straights.
Vessels far out
quietly fatiguing decks.
The breakers break
open to lost tidings.
Mariners cling biting
to the deck.

I
Do not know who
would want this
whatever it is
coming forth
out of this
and is among
and on either
side and
even above and
below these sands
and snows.

Repeating
Myself
as the earth does
and does not.

What
Are these ends
I come close to,
ends of everything
and nothing.
A profile is
seen a little
way off, with feeling.
And proliferates
independently
finding itself in
position, close or near
enough to act upon
some other thing.

For
This it is easy.
Unrelenting and
strangely incurious.
Hear, as you do,
these sounds in
the market place
of the outside tables of the
bar
rise to the open windows'
fractures.

Scratched
By a sand
speck, likely
possibility.

Not
Qualified.
Not so much
refusing
a word like
imagination
but establishing
a usable definition.
Image irrelevant.

Difficult
To take the land
as it changes
to the eye and ear
without the political
backing of the
intruder.

You
Do not weaken
in your resolve neither
to invent nor disregard.

What
Brought you here
in such elegiac
memory and splendid
elegance. You were
both mythic and
contemporary with
your presence
in the moment. In
both ways there were
teachers whose lessons
to mislead you
finally fell to
deaf ears. This was the
moment when you
established yourself
and disappeared
forever and forever.

    Altering
Position with the flight
of the bird
across the path
of the car. Attention
wavering or slowing
down, not until the last
moment, suddenly
the realization of
velocities
banking on hopes
revolving, winging
velocities. What,
but, if the whole
chirpy enterprise just
stops, fleetingly,
away from the wheels,
weakening.

    Distinguishing
The dewberry in
its bramble crossings
shape of the glass
shape of the writing
shape of the mind
not distinguishing.
Looking into the
distance, shape of
the strength. They
think nothing is the matter,
that it should be so, that
is all.

Not
To waste what
is available
or question
sour survival
—not to be sour
but, hardly
sweetened, either,
to the waking
response of a
very forgotten
language and
what is said
in this abstraction
between mountain
and mountain, straight
in the eye.

And
Save me too
your introductions.
Watch the sea
move in first
lapping round your
groyne, then lashing
the wall and
out again.

A
Scrap of bank paper
marking the
place
took off
at the pages
fluttering
like a butterfly.

Convalescent
Concaulescence
kept us
coming
apart.

If
The media is jerky
it is because it is
full of jerks.

People
Assembling
into assessments.
Persuasive people
capable of dissembling.

The
Air
resounding with
the heaviness of
the rotor blades
as you sit
with a lace collar—
it does not explain
composure—
it is your head
supporting your fist.

This
Utterly un-
acceptable ceiling.

I
Love you
in your field.

What
Is the trajectory
of the perfect scythe.

What
Question eludes
the scriptures
and the emptiness
closed and close
to the time
the interruptions
evolved
wearing into the age
of breath and
rays.

Some
Tiny mechanisms
working better
than those who
do not seem
to work
died in the dish
in the unknown
wherewith
some began
the way
to start up
in unanswerable
citation.

A
Cutting edge
at every point
displaces figures
of inadequacy.
Phasic
afinality.

Every
Day they connive
at encouraging
every dear
bit of dung
emotion taking the
position occupied
in an ablaut-series
by one particular
bowel.

The
Forging of outlandish
policies.

There
Is nothing strange
in coincidence.

A
Legitimate aspiration
has been hindered
by a silence
uncounting in the eternal.

Some
Brilliance
like a bird of prey
above the white
beam.

"Ruhe auf der Flucht."

AN UNCOLLECTED POEM

IN A RADIANT GARDEN

for E Y

When I think how lovely you are
with these hanging gardens, how
sick, how tired, I have grown of
upturned hills cleared of poetry.

It dawns on you. Flushed apples
picked out on a rosewood slat
in the autumn light. The sun
shines through your eyes.

Gardens are filled with needs.
Friendly willows sweep across.
You fold up your black clothes
and take on colour.

INDEX OF TITLES OR FIRST LINES

A billow 138
Absent 69
A/Cutting edge 369
After 101
After bloodspring 98
A lady bird 222
A/Legitimate aspiration 371
A light rainfall. 112
Along the edge of hedgerows. 224
Also/Now no 342
Altering/Position with the flight 364
A marriage 11
Ana 55
An aeolian scarecrow 227
An/Ancient play 312
And/Finding 348
And/Save me too 365
And/Slowly 308
And the Red Shift 19
And/When the words 324
An Imaginary Conversation 21
Animate 204
A/Plantation 318
Apodal Stride (Cursive) 74
A sandstone mountain appeared. 135
A/Scrap of bank paper 366
A single crow 121
As the Light, So the Cold 205
As/The others weave. 328
At Night 203
At/Rest like 359
Atrocities 203
At the back of the throat 224
A/Walk through 331
A White Mess 259
A/Wishbone 351
Ay 154

Bas showing 223
Because/I am the well- 354
Before Language 164
Before this history 93
Before us 147
Below the field of fleshy oat 118
Benedicte 169
Bit/Between the teeth 359
Black Art 20
Blake or Yeats Slept With You 241
Bombs and fires 223
Broad/Scapes from everything 320
Burning ears 254
But/Somewhere there 319

Cadence 197
Cancelled 163
Cat and kitten. 246
Catastrophic 199
Celan 51

Changing/Voices changing 310
Claim Song 172
Clarity 195
Clearly, and Not at Great Length 78
Cloisters 53
Clouds race. 127
Codicil 61
Collision 154
Come 184
Coming at an end 129
Coming/Into algae 322
Committed 189
Complaint 171
Cone 154
Conical rosewood 217
Consequences 193
Continued 22
Convalescent/Concaulescence 366
Cool/I was cool 335
Crisis 201
Crossing 72
Crux 50
Crystal/Beyond yellow. 313

Darkness 193
Dead 173
Death 73
Decisive 188
Definite Poem 23
Desert rose, desert rose, 121
Determined to make this long 238
Different/Creatures weathering 308
Difficult/To take the land 362
Dispersed/Between the 326
Distinguishing/The dewberry in 364
Disturbed/By an inevitable 355
Does the whole world revolve around 213
Do not imagine 93
Do/People change— 328
Do these lines ever meet. 226
Do you think I am a stone, 90
Drops 65

East 157
Emotion 17
Empty/Phrases, lost applications, 311
Endangered Species 185
Entropy 180
Every/Day they connive 370
Everything/You did not want 343

Fail. 148
False 56
Far 195
Feeling as if you had recognized 239
Fell 186
Flying/Away and 303

Flying/Through space 304
For/The bear 343
For/This it is easy. 361
Fractions. Eying 224
Fragile & Lucid 83
Fragment I 170
Fragment II 170
Fragment III 170
Frozen 179

Gentle phases of the moon 256
Give/Me a landscape 352

Habeas Corpus 68
Half/Ambition 317
He could guess 146
Here/In the unspeakable 345
Here/O Israel— 335
Here, roughly, 113
He was pleased but could not easily
    follow, 145
History 158
Hommage nul 200
Hot 155
How close is this wound, 98
How/Has age 311
How/I longed for 305
How will you know when the water
    tower 228
How you grow. 111

I am abstract 88
I am bound in this leaf state. 92
I am cold. 87
I am for life. 222
I am thinking about 109
I and They in Disagreement 161
I and this vastness 89
I Assure You 196
I Began 192
I Believe You 194
I bite too hard 119
I/Cannot hide 326
Ice, Fire 59
I/Do not know who 360
I/Do not seem to know 347
I do not speak of it. 233
I/Do not want 334
I don't hold a red candle up to you.
    218
I/Drink stone-fruit 341
If/It is possible 344
If/The media is jerky 366
If you saw me now 216
If/You wrote 304
'I haven't the least idea.' Nor I. 225
I hear about such things. 117
I/Hold an 332

I knew certain 144
I know this place 110
I lean across you 96
I look at the two girls 124
I/Love you 368
I love your stocky, 214
Imperfect/As in the nature 354
Imperfect Faith 190
In a Radiant Garden 375
Indistinct Voices 182
In doubt I trust. 214
In Green and Blue 90
In haste 119
In Peace 15
In/Resigning 306
Inside 246
In/The evening 358
In the night, 256
In/The Settlement 318
In the track of whales singing. 126
In/The wide sweep 351
In this 87
In this Green and Blue 87
Intonation 165
In/Working to 353
I/Raise myself 319
I remember the wind— 233
I rub out all that this vastness 91
I spit orange. 91
I/Stayed to 336
It/Is easy 332
It is evening. The labiates spread 238
It/Is formulated 352
It is troublesome to search 95
I/Turn 307
I turn against you 91
It was a crow 122
I walk from day to day 94
I/Was here 310
I wish you would 112

January 185

Lace-edged, 229
Ledge 162
Let/Inessentials pass. But 333
Level 164
Life, Loss 188
Light/Bursting 323
Lightning and thunder. 227
. . . Like/Those gone 338
Look at leaf. 222
Look/For the pure 337
Looking Around 158
Loss of Consciousness 20
Lost/Face awaiting 316

Mahler's Incurable Heart Disease 21

Maladjust 164
Masks 54
Memory 71
  Mica. 249
  More/Than once 314
  Mother of eye 232
Movement 188
Moving Buildings 291
  Mud settles. 109
Museum and Park 66
Musical Chairs 165
My Daughter's Brought a Good Man
    Home 79

  Naked/in long grass 230
  Naked/in long grasses 229
Neither to Disparage Nor Flatter You
    200
  New/Glue replaced 346
Nitrogen Narcosis 155
  No blue is crossed out 237
  No/Oceanic occasion 329
Not Godlike 176
  Nothing stirs. 128
  Not/Qualified. 362
  Not/To avoid the 321
  Not/To call up 315
  Not/To examine 320
  Not/To waste what 365
  Not/Yet lips of the world 344
  Nought now inspires. 216

  Oars, 228
  Of/All that was 338
  Of human hypocrisy 141
One 24
  One light stares out, 113
  One morning 149
  On/The condition 327
Orchestra 67

Packing 153
Paper 153
Parting of the Ways 169
Pass 181
Peace 198
  Peg of drift wood. 247
Penitent 202
  People/Assembling 367
  Petals fall 233
  Petals/Sprinkled 331
Phrasal 197
Pines 159
Planets 183
Poem 25
Poem 182
Poem About Music 29
  Poised/For what incredible angles.
    317

Poland's Neighbouring Cottage 299
Positioning 197
Powerless 199
  Practically/In this leaning 310
  Practically/The only thing left 325
Praise 15
Prologue 15
Protestation 157
Psalm 183
Psychological Mobbing 162

Quest 182

Random 189
  Rape stalks are laid 115
  Reach me. 134
  Red/Blotches, rashes, 341
Refusal to Know More Than You 187
  Remembering/Where I had 350
Remonstrate 173
  Repeating/Myself 360
  Residual cover, 79
Rich and Peachy 16
Ruins 198

  Scratched/By a sand 362
  Scythe. You implant the long curved
      blade. 110
Sham 189
  Silvery/Light on the 312
  Since it is like a leaf, 114
  Sitting/Still above 348
Sleep 67
  Smell/Of the Gymnosperm 358
  Smoke/And the sparrows 305
  Smoke from the factory rises 80
  Snow falls every day, 97
Snyflung 166
  Some/Brilliance 371
  Some days I sought shelter 133
Some Scandal that Has Floated Down
    from Higher Circles 77
  Some/Tiny mechanisms 369
  Speak 143
Speaking 174
  Spines grow out 122
Spirit Is Renewed 186
  Statutory./A heavy weariness 347
  Storming/Inexpectant 356
Strings 163
  Sucked/By the lips 309
  Suddenly/There is a seating 324

  Takes/The edge away 303
Target 175
  The/Ages of reading the 340
  The/Air 367
The Almond 178
The Arduous Meadow 177

The Arrival   22
  The/Blue the   330
  The boat in the distance   125
The Book of Mysteries   57
  The bovine horn   253
  The burn from the glowing   245
  The bush is shapped like a cupped
    hand.   109
  The chatter, chatter   211
The City   52
The Continental Drift   18
  The/Crop spray chemical   327
  The curves,   252
  The day dawned, and held   137
The Edge of the Land   191
  The effects   221
  The eye clouds.   248
  The eyes startle   115
  The ferry boat comes out of the mist
    fast.   96
  The fish coughs.   231
  The fish is double.   231
  The foliage is not vast,   88
  The/Forging of outlandish   370
  The gathering of dust.   245
  The gulls cry inland; the   80
  The history of theatre   90
  The house at odds.   255
  The leaves in the tea are   123
The Letter   196
The Lie   58
  The meaning of my dream   95
  The/Metropolis   356
  The morning come, they   136
  The music   255
  The night stares out   114
  Then/In naming   336
  Then light fails.   92
The Occasional Memory   17
  The/Opaque language   345
The Palace   70
The Pipe Organ Builders   265
  The/Power of those   340
  The rain brings down.   252
  There are many.   128
  There/Are times   344
  There is no end to it.   129
  There/Is nothing strange   370
  The/Rock over   330
  The rose stays in the cold.   116
  These/Reproductions   342
The Seventeenth of May   179
  The small verse   94
  The/Sound carries   353
The Spelling   18
The Stolen Analogy   19
  The/Sudden change   334
  The summer berries   118

  The/Table has dipped   339
  The traffic light switches   123
  The/True critic   349
  The/Truet   306
The Unpardonable   174
  The wasp   110
  The/Way you talk   338
  The weak must bear   142
  The wind is stuck here.   247
  The wind stops   226
  The world is a half terrible place,   117
  They are mostly   140
  They/Are the same   350
  The yellow flame surprises.   126
  They see a stranger,   139
  This poem is also for you.   120
  This/Utterly un-   367
  This/Will simply   307
  Through/Wrought iron   349
  Thrust/Upon one   308
Thy Dæmon   166
  Time is a kind   89
To Reassure, To   68
  To write down what you hear   232
Track   180
Trauma   180
True Meaning   185
  True voices   89
Turn   181
Two   24

Under the light   120

Veifa   184
  Victory is not subdued.   92

Waves   204
  Waves/Of electronic   346
  We are pushed.   210
Weights   191
  We lay down.   150
  We let the water stagnate.   251
We May Be Told to Go   16
  What/Are these ends   361
  What/Brought you here   363
  Whatever/Efficacy turns   357
  What is poetry?   251
  What is so strange.   111
  What/Is the trajectory   368
  What is you   93
  What/Lies between   325
  What/Question eludes   368
  When I look out on the world   116
  When I see you I want to kiss   239
  When/I wanted us   314
  When/My dear you are   337
  When/The language   323
  When the pipes enter   250

When/Three dimensions 322
Where/Shall I turn to 357
Which/Fence face fire 315
Will you kiss my sweetness? 209
Window of Air 156
With all the care in the world 124
With You 66
With Your Broadness and Your Tightness 192
Woman Spoke 49

X 230

You 187
You 250
You and I in Agreement 161
You and I stole circa 2000 kroner from I. 215
You are the last frame 95
You are the waiter. 127
You Break 184
You can. 209
You/Cannot recognize this 329

You die in this 88
You do not believe 225
You/Do not come 309
You do not see them. 125
You/Do not weaken 363
You/Draw things 316
You/Know I cannot 321
You/Know that 339
You/Lift the knee 331
You must listen to what is said. 97
You/Press the 333
Your Ambition 192
Your Demand 194
Your hands are beautiful! 212
Your sharp stresses 94
You See Through Me 196
You/Sense something wrong 333
You speak 60
You've done it now. 210
You/Were dispossessed 313
You were not trying to drag anybody into the gutter, 237
Y quién clama las doce no son trece. 211